THE NATIONAL COUNCIL OF TEACHERS OF MATHEMATICS

THE THIRTEENTH YEARBOOK

THE NATURE OF PROOF

A DESCRIPTION AND EVALUATION OF CERTAIN PROCEDURES
USED IN A SENIOR HIGH SCHOOL TO DEVELOP AN UNDER-
STANDING OF THE NATURE OF PROOF

By HAROLD P. FAWCETT, PH.D.

BUREAU OF PUBLICATIONS
TEACHERS COLLEGE, COLUMBIA UNIVERSITY
NEW YORK CITY
1938

THE NATIONAL COUNCIL OF TEACHERS OF MATHEMATICS, INC.
1906 Association Drive, Reston, VA 20191-9988
(703) 620-9840; (800) 235-7566; www.nctm.org

Originally published in 1938

Second printing 1995
Third printing 2001
Fourth printing 2004

ISBN 0-87353-402-6

Printed in the United States of America

EDITOR'S PREFACE

THIS is the thirteenth of a series of Yearbooks which the National Council of Teachers of Mathematics began to publish in 1926. The titles of the first twelve Yearbooks are as follows:

1. A Survey of Progress in the Past Twenty-Five Years.
2. Curriculum Problems in Teaching Mathematics.
3. Selected Topics in the Teaching of Mathematics.
4. Significant Changes and Trends in the Teaching of Mathematics Throughout the World Since 1910.
5. The Teaching of Geometry.
6. Mathematics in Modern Life.
7. The Teaching of Algebra.
8. The Teaching of Mathematics in the Secondary School.
9. Relational and Functional Thinking in Mathematics.
10. The Teaching of Arithmetic.
11. The Place of Mathematics in Modern Education.
12. Approximate Computation.

The present study is one in which interest has already been aroused all over the country through the desire of teachers to find a way not only to teach the important facts of geometry but also to acquaint the pupil with the kinds of thinking one needs in life situations which can best be learned by a study of geometry.

I wish to express my personal appreciation as well as that of the National Council of Teachers of Mathematics to Professor H. P. Fawcett for permitting us to publish this contribution to mathematical education as the Thirteenth Yearbook of the series.

W. D. REEVE

THE NATIONAL COUNCIL OF TEACHERS
OF MATHEMATICS

The National Council of Teachers of Mathematics is a national organization of mathematics teachers whose purpose is to:

1. Create and maintain interest in the teaching of mathematics.
2. Keep the values of mathematics before the educational world.
3. Help the inexperienced teacher to become a good teacher.
4. Help teachers in service to become better teachers.
5. Raise the general level of instruction in mathematics.

Anyone interested in mathematics is eligible to membership in the National Council upon payment of the annual dues of $2.00. The dues include subscription to the official journal of the Council (*The Mathematics Teacher*). Correspondence should be addressed to *The Mathematics Teacher*, 525 West 120th Street, New York City.

ACKNOWLEDGMENTS

No piece of research is the work of any one individual, and I wish to acknowledge my indebtedness to all those who have assisted either directly or indirectly in the development of this study. I recognize my obligation to those men and women whose researches have directed attention to neglected educational values. I am grateful to Professor W. D. Reeve for his sympathetic and stimulating interest; to Professor Helen Walker for her encouragement and valuable suggestions concerning the presentation of this material; to Dr. Lou LaBrant whose friendly counsel was most helpful in the organization of the study; to Dr. L. E. Raths, Dr. M. L. Hartung, and Dr. J. E. Wert whose willing and unselfish cooperation made possible the evaluation. My thanks and appreciation are extended to all these people but I feel that my greatest obligation is to the pupils whose enthusiasm was a constant source of inspiration and without whom this most enjoyable experience would have been impossible.

H.P.F.

CONTENTS

CHAPTER I

INTRODUCTION

THE GENERAL NATURE OF THE PROBLEM

THERE has probably never been a time in the history of American education when the development of critical and reflective thought was not recognized as a desirable outcome of the secondary school. Within recent years, however, this outcome has assumed increasing importance and has had a far-reaching effect on the nature of the curriculum. Teachers in all areas have felt the effect of this change in emphasis and their general acceptance of it has been accompanied by an increasing modification of classroom procedures. Teachers of mathematics, however, have felt that this new emphasis called for little change in their field since demonstrative geometry has long been justified on the ground that its chief contribution to the general education of the young people in our secondary schools is to acquaint them with the nature of deductive thought and to give them an understanding of what it really means to prove something. While verbal allegiance is paid to these large general objectives related to the nature of proof, actual classroom practice indicates that the major emphasis is placed on a body of theorems to be learned rather than on the *method* by which these theorems are established. The pupil feels that these theorems are important in themselves and in his earnest effort to "know" them he resorts to memorization. The tests most commonly used emphasize the importance of factual information, and there is little evidence to show that pupils who have studied demonstrative geometry are less gullible, more logical and more critical in their thinking than those who did not follow such a course.

It is the purpose of this study to describe classroom procedures by which geometric proof may be used as a means for cultivating critical and reflective thought and to evaluate the effect of such experiences on the thinking of the pupils.

THE ORIGIN AND BACKGROUND OF THE PROBLEM

The history of mathematical education in the United States reveals the fact that demonstrative geometry was taught only in colleges until a comparatively recent date. Whatever the values derived from the study of this subject may have been they were reserved for the selected group of young men and women who were interested in continuing their formal education beyond that offered in the public school. However, as new and interesting subjects claimed the attention of those responsible for college curricula it gradually developed that there was no room in these curricula for demonstrative geometry, while the rapid and increasing development of the secondary school presented an opportunity for continued study of this subject.[1] It thus happened that by the middle of the nineteenth century demonstrative geometry became a definite part of the high school curriculum, but with the change in the maturity of the pupils to whom this work was offered there occurred no fundamental change in the nature of the content. In considering the teaching of geometry John Wesley Young writes, "Our texts in this subject are still patterned more or less closely after the model of Euclid, who wrote over two thousand years ago, and whose text, moreover, was not intended for the use of boys and girls, but for mature men."[2]

It is true that teachers of mathematics recognized the advisability of so modifying the subject matter as to make it more palatable to the less mature pupils in the secondary schools and a number of important committees[3] have studied

[1] A complete and thorough treatment of the significant changes and trends in the teaching of geometry may be found in *The History of the Teaching of Elementary Geometry* by Alvin W. Stamper, Bureau of Publications, Teachers College, Columbia University, 1909, and in *Recent Developments in the Teaching of Geometry* by J. Shibli, Pennsylvania State College, State College, Pennsylvania, 1932.

[2] John Wesley Young, *Lectures on Fundamental Concepts of Algebra and Geometry*, p. 1. The Macmillan Co., New York, 1925.

[3] Committee of Ten on Secondary School Studies, 1894.
Committee on College Entrance Requirements, 1899.
National Committee of Fifteen on Geometry Syllabus, 1912.
National Committee on Mathematical Requirements, 1923.
College Entrance Examination Board. Document 108, 1923.
First Committee on Geometry, 1929.
Second Committee on Geometry, 1930.
Third Committee on Geometry, 1932.

this problem. As a result many theorems have disappeared from modern texts, different arrangements of those remaining have been suggested, new theorems have been introduced, and methods of teaching have changed; but in general there has been no significant change in the nature of the subject matter. The great majority of geometry students, regardless of their interests and capacities, are required to work through ninety or more theorems selected by the author of the particular text used in any given situation. Certain properties of geometric figures are assumed and the student is asked to establish other predetermined properties by logical proof.

THE VALUES CLAIMED FOR DEMONSTRATIVE GEOMETRY

The subject matter relates to rectilinear figures, circles, proportion and areas. After the pupil has covered the allotted number of theorems and has demonstrated his ability to work out a number of original exercises, it is assumed that the values to be derived from the study of demonstrative geometry have been added to his educational equipment. What are these values? What is the unique contribution which demonstrative geometry makes to the general education of the young people in our secondary schools? The National Committee on the Reorganization of Mathematics in Secondary Education answers this question by saying that purposes of instruction in this subject are: "To exercise further the spatial imagination of the student, to make him familiar with the great basal propositions and their applications, to develop understanding and appreciation of a deductive proof and the ability to use this method of reasoning where it is applicable, and to form habits of precise and succinct statement, of the logical organization of ideas, and of logical memory."[4] This important question has also been discussed by many of the leading teachers in the field of mathematics. While it is not possible to quote all of the answers which have been made, some of the most significant are presented here.

In the Fifth Yearbook of the National Council, Professor Reeve writes that "The purpose of geometry is to make clear to the pupil the meaning of demonstration, the meaning of

[4] National Committee on Mathematical Requirements, *The Reorganization of Mathematics in Secondary Education* (Part i), p. 48. Houghton Mifflin Co., Boston, 1923.

mathematical precision, and the pleasure of discovering absolute truth. If demonstrative geometry is not taught in order to enable the pupil to have the satisfaction of proving something, to train him in deductive thinking, to give him the power to prove his own statements, then it is not worth teaching at all."[5*]

In similar vein Professors Birkhoff and Beatley of Harvard University say that "In demonstrative geometry the emphasis is on reasoning. . . . To the extent that the subject fails to develop the power to reason and to yield an appreciation of scientific method in reasoning, its fundamental value for purposes of instruction is lessened."[6]

The Third Committee on Geometry of which Professor Beatley is chairman reports that "Teachers agree that the main outcomes of demonstrative geometry pertain to logical thinking and wish to maintain the distinction between this subject and informal geometry which emphasizes the factual aspects of geometry. . . . There is equally enthusiastic response to the proposal that instruction in demonstrative geometry call attention to logical chains of theorems, to the gaps in Euclid's logic and bring the pupil to appreciate the nature of a mathematical system, the need of undefined terms, the arbitrariness of assumptions and the possibility of other arrangements of propositions than that given in his own text."[7]

In discussing this problem Dr. H. C. Christofferson says, "Geometry achieves its highest possibilities if, in addition to its direct and practical usefulness, it can establish a pattern of reasoning; if it can develop the power to think clearly in geometric situations, and to use the same discrimination in non-geometric situations; if it can develop the power to generalize with caution from specific cases, and to realize the force and all-inclusiveness of deductive statements; if it can develop an appreciation of the place and function of defini-

[5] W. D. Reeve, "The Teaching of Geometry," *Fifth Yearbook of the National Council of Teachers of Mathematics*, 1930, pp. 13–14.

*Hereinafter the *Yearbooks of the National Council of Teachers of Mathematics* will be referred to as *Yearbook*.

[6] G. D. Birkhoff and Ralph Beatley, "A New Approach to Elementary Geometry," *Fifth Yearbook*, 1930, p. 86.

[7] Ralph Beatley, "The Third Report of the Committee on Geometry," *The Mathematics Teacher*, Vol. xxviii, No. 6, 1935, p. 334.

tions and postulates in the proof of any conclusion, geometric or non-geometric; if it can develop an attitude of mind which tends always to analyze situations, to understand their inter-relationships, to question hasty conclusions, to express clearly, precisely, and accurately non-geometric as well as geometric ideas."[8]

As a final contribution to this discussion let us consider the clear and forceful statement of Professor C. B. Upton who says, "I firmly believe that the reason we teach demonstrative geometry in our high schools today is to give pupils certain ideas about the nature of proof. The great majority of teachers of geometry hold this same point of view. Some teachers may at first think our purpose in teaching geometry is to acquaint pupils with a certain body of geometric facts or theorems, or with the applications of these theorems in everyday life, but on second reflection they will probably agree that our great purpose in teaching geometry is to show pupils how facts are proved. I will go still further in clarifying our aims. . . . The purpose in teaching geometry is not only to acquaint pupils with the methods of proving geometric facts, but also to familiarize them with that rigorous kind of thinking which Professor Keyser has so aptly called 'the If-Then kind, a type of thinking which is distinguished from all others by its characteristic form: If this is so, then that is so.' Our great aim in the tenth year is to teach the nature of deductive proof and to furnish pupils with a model of all their life thinking."[9] Professor Keyser calls this kind of thinking "autonomous thinking" or "postulational thinking" and proceeds to point out that in the "Elements" of Euclid we find "The most famous example of autonomous thought in the history of science."[10]

It is noticeable that in these statements concerning the chief contribution which the study of demonstrative geometry makes to the general education of young people very little, if any, reference is made to the facts of geometry. The truth of the matter is that demonstrative geometry is no longer

[8] H. C. Christofferson, *Geometry Professionalized for Teachers*, p. 28. George Banta Publishing Co., Menasha, Wis., 1933.

[9] C. B. Upton, "The Use of Indirect Proof in Geometry and Life," *Fifth Yearbook*, 1930, pp. 131–132.

[10] C. J. Keyser, *Thinking about Thinking*, p. 25. E. P. Dutton and Co., New York, 1926.

justified on the ground that it is necessary for the purpose of giving students control of useful geometric knowledge, since the facts of geometry which may at one time or another actually serve some useful purpose in the developing life of a boy or girl are learned or can be learned in the junior high school. In the "Third Report of the Committee on Geometry" already quoted, the committee states, "It is generally agreed that the important facts of geometry can be mastered below the tenth grade through inductions based on observation, measurement, constructions with drawing instruments, cutting and pasting, and also through simple deductions from the foregoing inductions as well as from geometric notions intuitively held."[11] The consensus of opinion therefore seems to be that the most important values to be derived from the study of demonstrative geometry are an acquaintance "with the nature of proof" and a familiarity with "postulational thinking" as a method of thought which is available, not only in the field of mathematics, but also "in every field of thought, in the physical sciences, in the moral or social sciences, in all matters and situations where it is important for men and women to have logically organized bodies of doctrine to guide them and save them from floundering in the conduct of life."[12]

GENERAL ACCEPTANCE OF THESE VALUES

These purposes are recognized as worthy and desirable, not only by teachers of mathematics but by most thoughtful men and women who are interested in the general education of young people. There is no disagreement concerning the educational value of any experience which leads children to recognize the necessity for clarity of definition, to weigh evidence, to look for the assumptions on which conclusions depend, and to understand what proof really means. John Dewey has defined reflective thinking as "active, persistent and careful consideration of any belief or supposed form of knowledge in the light of the grounds that support it and the further conclusions to which it tends."[13] And in view of the

[11] Ralph Beatley, *op. cit.*, p. 334.
[12] C. J. Keyser, *op. cit.*, p. 35.
[13] John Dewey, *How We Think*, p. 6. D. C. Heath and Co., Boston, 1910.

stated purposes for teaching demonstrative geometry is it not reasonable to expect that effective work in the study of this subject should lead the pupil to examine critically any conclusion he is pressed to accept "in the light of the grounds that support it and the further conclusions to which it tends"? The "reflective thinking" of our young people should be improved through experience in analyzing situations which involve "the nature of proof."

The Columbia Associates in Philosophy have stated that "The function of education, in large part, is the moulding of minds capable of taking and using the best that the world has given. Such minds must be well stored with information, free from prejudice, critical of new ideas presented, and fitted to understand the kind and quantity of proof required before they may adopt the pronouncements of the generals of the society of minds."[14] While one might question the use of the word "moulding" in connection with an educational process, is there any subject in the curriculum of the secondary school which should make a greater contribution toward the development of minds that are "fitted to understand the kind and quantity of proof required" in the acceptance of conclusions than that subject which has as its fundamental purpose the leading of the student to understand what it really means to prove something?

ACHIEVEMENT OF VALUES QUESTIONED

The reasons which mathematicians offer to justify the continued teaching of demonstrative geometry to the young people in our secondary schools are not questioned so far as their educational value is concerned. There is, however, serious question as to whether or not these desirable results are actually achieved through the usual course in this subject. After a careful and thorough analysis of the results in the December "Every Pupil Plane Geometry Test" for Ohio, Dr. H. C. Christofferson writes, "The reasons given by pupils for statements often seem to disregard entirely the thought of the situation. Often it seems that it is mere habit that dictates the response, not a thought process. Pupils have often used

[14] Columbia Associates in Philosophy, *An Introduction to Reflective Thinking*, p. 11. Houghton Mifflin Co., Boston, 1923.

the various theorems as reasons and with satisfaction. They seem in some cases to have used them so often without meaning that they give them as so many memorized non-sense syllables. Guesses would be right more often than the type of reasoning attempted in some cases."[15] This statement would seem to indicate that the study of demonstrative geometry has not greatly improved the ability of the students to reason accurately even within the narrow confines of the subject. In view of this is it reasonable to expect that the results of such study will be more helpful in non-geometric situations?

The Third Committee on Geometry, composed of twenty-six prominent teachers in the field of mathematics, prepared a questionnaire which raised pertinent questions concerning the teaching of geometry.[16] This questionnaire was sent to each member of the committee and also to 101 of the outstanding teachers in Maine, Massachusetts, Ohio, Illinois, Minnesota, Kansas, Oklahoma and Colorado. The replies indicate that "there is almost unanimous agreement that demonstrative geometry can be so taught that it will develop the power to reason logically more readily than other school subjects, and that the degree of transfer of this logical training to situations outside geometry is a fair measure of the efficacy of the instruction. However great the partisan bias in this expression of opinion, the question 'Do teachers of geometry ordinarily teach in such a way as to secure transfer of those methods, attitudes, and appreciations which are commonly said to be most easily transferable?' elicits an almost unanimous but sorrowful 'No.'"[17]

A more vigorous statement concerning the outcomes of demonstrative geometry is made by Eric Bell in a recent volume in which he writes, "A diluted sort of Euclid . . . is one of the main-stays of American education today. It is supposed to quicken the reason, and there is no doubt that it does in the hands of a thoroughly competent and modernized teacher, who lets the children use their heads and see for them-

[15] H. C. Christofferson, *A State Wide Survey of the Learning and Teaching of Geometry*, p. 41. State Department of Education, Columbus, Ohio, 1930.
[16] Ralph Beatley, "The Second Report of the Committee on Geometry," *The Mathematics Teacher*, Vol. xxvi, No. 6, 1933, p. 366.
[17] Ralph Beatley, "The Third Report of the Committee on Geometry," *The Mathematics Teacher*, Vol. xxviii, No. 6, 1935, p. 336.

selves exactly how nonsensical some of the stuff presented as 'proof' really is. . . . Uncritical reverence for the supposed rigidity of Euclid's geometry had much to do with the retardation of progress in close reasoning. . . . If school children fail to get some conception of geometry and close reasoning out of their course in 'geometry' they get nothing, except possibly a permanent inability to think straight and a propensity to jump at conclusions which nothing in reason or sanity warrants."[18]

Now it is probably safe to assume that the values emphasized in the testing program of any school are those values which receive emphasis in the classroom, and a study of commonly used tests in geometry is sufficient to reveal that little, if any, attempt is made to measure the degree to which the purposes claimed for demonstrative geometry are realized. Perhaps the tests which have the widest use are the College Entrance Board Examinations, the Breslich Geometry Survey Test, the Cooperative Mathematics Tests, and the mathematics section of the Sones-Harry High School Achievement Test. It is claimed that together these tests are given to more than two million young people, which means that these students are being examined on the facts and skills of geometry, as there is little, if anything, in these tests which by any stretch of the imagination could be interpreted as examining children on their understanding of "the nature of proof" and their ability to apply postulational thinking to "situations outside the field of geometry."

The chief objective of mathematical study, according to Young,[19] is "to make the pupil think" and "if mathematical teaching fails to do this, it fails altogether." Young then continues with the following significant statement: "The mere memorizing of a demonstration in geometry has about the same educational value as the memorizing of a page from the city directory. And yet it must be admitted that a very large number of our pupils do study mathematics in just this way. There can be no doubt that the fault lies with the teaching."

[18] Eric Bell, *The Search for Truth*, pp. 124–126. Williams and Wilkins Co., Baltimore, 1934.
[19] John Wesley Young, *op. cit.*, pp. 4–5.

The assumption which mathematics teachers are making is that since demonstrative geometry offers possibilities for the development of critical thinking, this sort of thinking is *necessarily* achieved through a study of the subject. Such an assumption has not been validated and the results of past experience indicate that it should be seriously questioned. To theorize concerning values which are believed to be the unique contribution of demonstrative geometry to the general education of young people is not a difficult matter, but to plan and carry out this program in such a way that these desired outcomes are actually realized is a problem which has not been squarely faced by teachers of mathematics.

THE PROBLEM DEFINED

While teachers of mathematics agree in general as to the unique contribution which the study of demonstrative geometry should make to the general education of young people, there may be some disagreement as to just what they mean by "the nature of proof." How is this concept defined? What is it that a pupil has learned when he understands what a proof really means? While some teachers of mathematics will answer this question in one way and some in another, the importance of the answer should not be overlooked for on it will depend the sort of activity going on in the classroom. For purposes of this study it is assumed that a pupil understands the nature of deductive proof when he understands:

1. The place and significance of undefined concepts in proving any conclusion.
2. The necessity for clearly defined terms and their effect on the conclusion.
3. The necessity for assumptions or unproved propositions.
4. That no demonstration proves anything that is not implied by the assumptions.

In speaking of this topic Young states as follows: "If we consider the nature of a deductive proof, we recognize at once that there must be a hypothesis. It is clear, then, that the starting point of any mathematical science must be a set of one or more propositions which remain entirely unproved. This is essential; without it a vicious circle is unavoidable. Similarly we may see that there must be some undefined terms. In order to define a term we must define it in terms of some other term or terms, the meaning of which is assumed known. In order to be strictly logical, therefore, a set of one or more terms must be left entirely undefined."[20] It is further assumed that a pupil who understands these things will also understand that the conclusions thus established can have universal validity only if the definitions and assumptions which imply these conclusions have universal validity. The conclusions are "true" only to the extent that the fundamental bases from which they were derived are "true." Truth is relative and not absolute.

While teachers of mathematics say they want the young people in our secondary schools to understand the nature of proof, that should not be and probably is not their total concern. What these teachers really want is not only that these young people should understand the nature of proof but that their way of life should show that they understand it. Of what value is it for a pupil to understand thoroughly what a proof means if it does not clarify his thinking and make him more "critical of new ideas presented"? The real value of this sort of training to any pupil is determined by its effect on his behavior, and for purposes of this study we shall assume that if he clearly understands these aspects of the nature of proof his behavior will be marked by the following characteristics:

1. He will select the significant words and phrases in any statement that is important to him and ask that they be carefully defined.
2. He will require evidence in support of any conclusion he is pressed to accept.
3. He will analyze that evidence and distinguish fact from assumption.
4. He will recognize stated and unstated assumptions essential to the conclusion.
5. He will evaluate these assumptions, accepting some and rejecting others.

[20] John Wesley Young, *op. cit.*, p. 3.

6. He will evaluate the argument, accepting or rejecting the conclusion.

7. He will constantly re-examine the assumptions which are behind his beliefs and which guide his actions.

While the total educational experience of the student in the secondary school should contribute and doubtless does to some extent contribute to the development of this kind of behavior, there seem to the writer to be possibilities in demonstrative geometry which no other subject offers. While Professor Young considers the subject matter of mathematics to be of importance he writes as follows: "still more important than the subject matter of mathematics is the fact that it exemplifies most typically, clearly and simply certain modes of thought which are of utmost importance to everyone."[21] In this area the concepts considered and the ideas studied are devoid of strong emotional content. The student's native ability to think is not stifled by prejudice or bias. He becomes conscious of the fact that his conclusions are determined by the definitions and assumptions which he, himself, makes and he recognizes the far-reaching effect of these basic ideas. He sees a method of thought applied to idealized concepts and "without that ideal, thinking is without a just standard for self criticism; it is without light upon its course; it is a wanderer like a vessel at sea without a compass or star."[22] The logical rigor of geometric proof illustrates the needed "ideal," and it is the purpose of this study to show that by placing the major emphasis on those aspects of demonstrative geometry which serve to illustrate the nature of proof and not on the factual content of the subject, it is possible to improve the reflective thinking of young people and to develop minds that are "critical of new ideas presented, and fitted to understand the kind and quantity of proof required before they may adopt the pronouncements of the generals of the society of minds."

It is not sufficient, however, to study only those situations wherein the concepts are idealized and "the material to be

[21] J. W. A. Young, *The Teaching of Mathematics*, pp. 17–18. Longmans, Green and Co., New York, 1924.

[22] C. J. Keyser, "The Human Worth of Rigorous Thinking," *The Mathematics Teacher*, Vol. xv, No. 1, 1922, pp. 1–5.

presented is simple and wholly unobscured by the emotions."[23]
If the kind of thinking which is to result from an understanding of the nature of proof is to be used in non-mathematical situations such situations must be considered during the learning process. Wheeler says that "No transfer will occur unless the material is learned in connection with the field to which transfer is desired. Isolated ideas and subjects do not integrate. Learning is not bond-forming. It is an orderly and organized process of differentiating general grasps of situations with respect to experience. The details emerge organized, as they differentiate from previous knowledge, in the face of new situations, not repeated ones."[24] Transfer is secured only by training for transfer and teachers of mathematics can no longer expect that the careful study of ninety or more geometric theorems will alone enable their students to distinguish between a sound argument and a tissue of nonsense.

William Betz, who made a comprehensive study of the problem of transfer with particular reference to geometry, presents in a summary the following findings and states that they "might well be incorporated in the creed and daily practice of every progressive teacher":

1. Training for transfer is a worth-while aim of instruction; from the standpoint of life it is the most important aim.
2. Transfer is not automatic. "We reap no more than we sow."
3. Every type of "specific" training, if it is to rise above a purely mechanical level, should be used as a vehicle for generalized experience.
4. "The cultivation of thinking is the central concern of education."[25]

It is thus evident that the general problem to be attacked consists of three related problems:

1. The problem of leading the pupil to understand the nature of deductive proof through the study of geometric situations.

2. The problem of generalizing this experience so that effective transfer will result.

[23] Eric T. Bell, "The Meaning of Mathematics," *Eleventh Yearbook*, p. 138, 1936.
[24] R. H. Wheeler, "The New Psychology of Learning," *Tenth Yearbook*, p. 239, 1935.
[25] William Betz, "The Transfer of Training with Particular Reference to Geometry," *Fifth Yearbook*, pp. 149–198, 1930.

3. The problem of evaluating the resulting change in the behavior of the student.

A SUMMARY OF RELATED STUDIES

It has become increasingly evident in the last twenty-five years that the teaching of demonstrative geometry in secondary schools must be greatly improved if the values claimed for it are to be realized. Efforts to effect this improvement have, to a large extent, been directed to a rearrangement of geometric theorems and this rearrangement has been logically developed from an adult point of view. In discussing this situation E. Russell Stabler points out among other things that "The sequence of theorems tends to be arranged to meet the logical or traditional requirements of the subject as seen by the author, and not with a view to obtaining the maximum amount of cooperation from the pupils in developing and appreciating the logical structure."[26] Furthermore, little attention has been given to changes in the nature of the content which are necessary if the habits of thought, which it is hoped will be developed through a study of this subject, are to transfer to non-geometric situations.

The results of an interesting and suggestive experiment related to this problem are reported by Elsie Parker.[27] Assuming that under favorable conditions transfer of training from one field of experience to another is possible, she set up a controlled experiment in an effort to answer the question, "Can pupils of geometry be taught to prove theorems more economically and effectively when trained to use consciously a technique of logical thinking; and furthermore, does such training, more than the usual method, increase the pupil's ability to analyze and see relationships in other non-geometrical situations?" In connection with this problem she says, "The traditional method of instruction has been to let the pupil discover for himself a method of reasoning which he thereafter uses without, in many cases, being aware of the fact that he is using that mode of procedure." The pupils in the experimental group studied the thought process used

---

[26] E. Russell Stabler, "Teaching an Appreciation of Mathematics: The Need of Reorganization in Geometry," *The Mathematics Teacher*, Vol. xxvii, No. 1, 1934, p. 37.

[27] Elsie Parker, "Teaching Pupils the Conscious Use of a Technique of Thinking," *The Mathematics Teacher*, Vol. xvii, No. 4, 1924, pp. 191–201.

in proving geometric theorems and gained some understanding of the nature of logical thought, while in the control group the theorems themselves were recognized as of major importance and little attention was given to the thought process involved in proving them.

In order to measure the results of such training original geometric theorems were given to the classes before and after their work with Miss Parker, and after presenting the results of her study she says, "These data would seem to offer conclusive evidence, in so far as one experiment can be considered to do so, that when pupils are taught to use consciously a technique of logical thinking, they try more varied methods of attack, reject erroneous suggestions more readily, and without becoming discouraged maintain an attitude of suspended judgment until the method has been shown to be correct. The data on the reasoning tests would seem to indicate that such training in logical thinking with the materials of geometry tends to carry over these methods of attack and these attitudes to other problem situations not concerned with geometry."

A second experiment related to learning in geometry is reported by Winona Perry.[28] In this experiment Miss Perry had two control divisions and one experimental division. In each control division the instruction was definitely guided by a textbook. In one of these divisions the book propositions were emphasized as of primary importance, while in the other the emphasis was placed on the proving of original exercises. No attention was given in either group to any particular method of thinking, and in each case the class was conducted by the question and answer method. In the experimental division the development of a technique in reasoning about the exercises of geometry was of major importance. This technique in reasoning emphasized the "if-then" type of thinking as well as the analytic method and even though non-mathematical subject matter was not included in the course Miss Perry found, among other things, that in the experimental group "the ability to solve problems non-mathematical in character was markedly improved, following the period of training in the solution of exercises in geometry.

[28] Winona Perry, *A Study in the Psychology of Learning in Geometry.* Bureau of Publications, Teachers College, Columbia University, 1925.

This increased ability was most noticeable as resulting from those tests more nearly similar to the type of reasoning emphasized in demonstrative geometry in form and in content." In dealing with the necessary training of teachers of geometry Dr. H. C. Christofferson[29] states, "There remains then the problem of securing still further professionalization of subject-matter with more emphasis on the fundamental pattern of teaching geometry as well as on the foundations of geometry, more actual contact with high-school geometry, and more attention to the system of formulated reasoning and its application to non-geometric as well as geometric situations." In order to suggest a solution for this problem he analyzes all the theorems and constructions in the Report of the National Committee on the Reorganization of Mathematics and on the basis of this analysis presents a list of "The Essential Constructions and Theorems of Geometry," "essential" being defined as "necessary for the proof of other propositions." Using these "essential" theorems as illustrative material, he then presents principles and methods of presentation which emphasize "the fundamental pattern of teaching geometry" and which, in his opinion, should result in the maximum of transfer to "non-geometric as well as geometric situations."

Now a teacher of geometry whose major interest is "to teach the nature of deductive proof and to furnish pupils with a model for all their life thinking" is not primarily interested in the factual aspects of the subject and has no fixed number of theorems which he feels must be covered. Furthermore, it is relatively unimportant for this purpose what theorems are covered since the deductive process by which they are established is illustrative of a method and the theorems are not important in themselves. However, in selecting these theorems from the large number available it would seem sensible to study those which contribute most effectively to an acquaintance with the important ideas of geometry and Dr. Christofferson's list of "Essential Theorems and Constructions" should prove particularly helpful for this purpose.

[29] H. C. Christofferson, *Geometry Professionalized for Teachers*, p. 2. George Banta Publishing Co., Menasha, Wis., 1933.

CHAPTER II

EXPERIMENTAL CONDITIONS AND DATA

PUPILS AND CLASS ORGANIZATION

THE plan usually followed in a research experiment is similar to that used in the studies of Miss Parker and Miss Perry, both of which were summarized in the preceding chapter. One or more control groups are selected and by means of intelligence tests and other criteria which are assumed to be applicable these groups are "matched" with an experimental group. With the exception of the factor to which the person conducting the experiment is directing his attention, all variables are assumed to be constant for each group and it is believed that any difference in the achievement of the experimental group as contrasted with the achievement of the control groups is due to the variable factor. The results are computed with apparent precision but there is serious question whether this appearance of accuracy is not misleading. Is the degree to which all variables are actually under control such as to warrant this precise measurement? Professor Reeve points out that "One major drawback of the experimental approach to the solution of a problem is that in many of the studies where this type of research is employed the experimental group always or nearly always wins."[1]

Comparable classes for any experiment should be chosen for their similarity in characteristics which are essential to the nature of the work in the experiment. For example, if two groups of children are alike in height, weight and color of hair one would not consider these two groups comparable for an experimental study in free writing. This study deals with the development of a kind of thinking which, in the opinion of the writer, is not typical of that encouraged in the formal school program. It is well known, however, that standardized tests of mental development and of mathe-

[1] William D. Reeve, "Research in Mathematics Education," *The Mathematics Teacher*, Vol. xxix, No. 1, 1936, p. 7.

matical skill test the ability of the student to do school work *of the kind to which he has been accustomed*, or, in other words, those tests consist of experiences which are typical of the conventional school program and cannot safely be used to prognosticate ability to do other types of work successfully. Dr. Paul A. Witty writes that "A vital need in education at present is a more sympathetic understanding of children and their problems. To achieve this, the intelligence test is helpful, but its usefulness is impaired when its results are considered to reveal a faculty or function unrelated to character traits and emotional stability, and indeed to the behavior of the total organism in situations requiring intelligent choice of action."[2]

In view of these considerations the use of control groups in this study has seemed of doubtful value. To present the picture of a process through which students may be led to understand certain aspects of the nature of proof both in mathematical and in non-mathematical situations does not require comparable groups of pupils. In fact, if the pupil is to have "the opportunity to reason about the subject matter of geometry in his own way,"[3] if the logical processes which are to guide the development of the work are to be "those of the student and not those of the teacher,"[3] the very nature of the group will affect both procedures, and outcomes and control groups, selected as they have been in most experimental research, have no place in such a program. Evaluation is not delayed until the end of a quarter or a semester or until a certain unit has been completed. Evaluation should not and cannot be separated from classroom procedures, for it affects these procedures and is inherent in them.

The pupils in the class used for this experimental work were not selected according to any set of criteria. The program of each of fifty pupils called for mathematics and the only factor which operated in determining the class into which each of these fifty pupils was placed was conflict in schedule.

---

[2] Paul A. Witty, "Intelligence: Its Nature, Development and Measurement." Chap. xvi of *Educational Psychology*, p. 481, by Charles E. Skinner. Prentice-Hall, New York, 1936.

[3] Refer to the four fundamental assumptions on which classroom procedures are based. See page 21.

It finally transpired that twenty-five of them were given to one teacher and the remaining twenty-five to another teacher. Class A was the group used for this study, while the teacher of Class B followed the usual course in formal demonstrative geometry. In all other respects the programs of these fifty pupils were the same. For reasons already considered, however, Class B was not recognized as a control group and any variation in achievement between the two groups with respect to values related to the nature of proof should be interpreted within the limitations of the situation.

These fifty pupils were not all members of the same grade. They were distributed through grades 9, 10 and 11 as shown in Table 1.

TABLE I

GRADE PLACEMENT OF PUPILS IN CLASSES A AND B

Year in School	Class A	Class B
Grade 9	3	0
Grade 10	7	8
Grade 11	15	17

There was an almost even distribution of boys and girls between the two classes as shown in Table 2.

TABLE 2

DISTRIBUTION OF BOYS AND GIRLS IN CLASSES A AND B

Sex	Class A	Class B
Girls	16	14
Boys	9	11

The average age of the pupils in Class A was slightly less than the average age of those in Class B. The distribution of the ages is given in Table 3.

TABLE 3

AGE OF PUPILS IN CLASSES A AND B

Age	Number in Class A	Number in Class B
18	0	1
17	1	3
16	13	12
15	5	6
14	2	2
13	4	1

None of these pupils had previously studied demonstrative geometry and the extent of their work in informal geometry varied with the individual pupil. All of them had completed a year in elementary algebra. The Otis intelligence scores of these pupils were available, and in Table 4 the range, the median and first and third quartiles for both groups are given.

TABLE 4

OTIS INTELLIGENCE SCORES OF PUPILS IN CLASS A AND B

	Class A	Class B
Range	91–133	94–140
First Quartile	110	102
Median	115	109
Third Quartile	125	121

Each of these classes met four times each week. The periods were forty minutes in length and this time was used at the discretion of the teacher for *all* class activities. No outside preparation was required of the pupils. These four periods each week included all needed study time, and while a number of pupils studied outside of class time they did so voluntarily. Frequent periods of supervised study made it possible for each pupil to work at whatever seemed most important to him and for the teacher to give individual help and guidance where needed. This program continued for a period of two school years covering sixty-eight weeks.

TYPES OF DATA

There are two types of data with which this study is mainly concerned. One type of primary importance consists of the methods and processes through which the pupils become familiar with postulational thinking and through which they gain some understanding of the nature of proof. These methods and processes, however, must be applied to certain content and it is this content which provides the second type of data.

DATA DEALING WITH METHODS AND PROCESSES

While it is recognized that methods and processes will vary and should vary with different students, it is also recognized that if they are to be effective they can be determined in no haphazard manner. The procedures used in this particular study are derived from four basic assumptions, as follows:

1. That a senior high school pupil has reasoned and reasoned accurately before he begins the study of demonstrative geometry.
2. That he should have the opportunity to reason about the subject matter of geometry in his own way.
3. That the logical processes which should guide the development of the work should be those of the pupil and not those of the teacher.
4. That opportunity should be provided for the application of the postulational method to non-mathematical material.

Raymond H. Wheeler, in discussing "the new psychology of learning," writes: "Learning is not exclusively an inductive process. First impressions are not chaotic and unorganized. . . . There is nothing more highly organized than children's logic, to which impressions are subordinate. Adults do not discover this logic, that is all."[4]

This quotation not only lends some support to the four basic assumptions just stated, but it also suggests that if the values claimed for demonstrative geometry are to be derived from a study of this subject, the "children's logic"

[4] Raymond H. Wheeler, "The New Psychology of Learning," *Tenth Yearbook*, pp. 237–238, 1935.

must be respected. According to present practice, however, these young people are given a text fashioned by an adult pattern of logic, and little, if any, opportunity is offered them to think about the content in their own way. As an introduction to the subject an effort is made to lead them to be suspicious of conclusions reached through observation and they are then faced with numerous generalizations which they are asked to accept without proof. These generalizations are called postulates and it is often pointed out that the truth of these postulates is "self-evident." Is there not an inconsistency in this approach to the study of proof? Is not "observation" involved in determining whether or not the truth of a generalization is "self-evident," and if one is to be "suspicious of conclusions reached through observation" why should the truth of these postulates be accepted as "self-evident"? This question might well be raised by any thoughtful pupil and the fact that it is not raised should cause teachers of geometry to question the effectiveness of their teaching.

Furthermore, this approach "instead of emphasizing the relative nature of the truth of geometry, emphasizes absolute truth. Instead of treating the postulates as a convenient starting point for the subject, it leads pupils to consider the postulates as inevitable truths,"[5] and imposes on them a pattern of thought determined by criteria which they do not accept as logical. Such practice tends to stifle the very outcomes claimed for the subject. "The trouble," according to John Wesley Young, "is that the authors of practically all of our current textbooks lay all the emphasis on the formal logical side, to the almost complete exclusion of the psychological, which latter is without doubt far more important at the beginning of a first course in algebra or geometry. They fail to recognize the fact that the pupil has reasoned, and reasoned accurately, on a variety of subjects before he takes up the subject of mathematics, though this reasoning has not perhaps been formal. In order to induce a pupil to think about geometry, it is first necessary to arouse his interest and then to let him think about the subject in his own way."[6]

[5] E. Russell Stabler, "Teaching an Appreciation of Mathematics: The Need of Reorganization in Geometry," *The Mathematics Teacher*, Vol. xxvii, No. 1, 1934, p. 35.
[6] John Wesley Young, *Lectures on Fundamental Concepts of Algebra and Geometry*, p. 5. The Macmillan Co., New York, 1925.

When this is done the spirit of discovery is encouraged and preserved, and there is little doubt that a pupil who discovers even a simple mathematical principle by his own efforts has had a most wholesome and truly educational experience.

In a most interesting discussion on "The Next Step in Method," Dr. William Heard Kilpatrick points out that "The most widespread and imperative present tendency along methodological lines is the insistent demand that we get our students more fully 'into the game'."[7] He then presents five possibilities, illustrating varying degrees of activity on the part of the pupils and these are:

1. A pupil memorizes the bare words of a demonstration.
2. A pupil memorizes the idea of a demonstration and can reproduce it in different words.
3. A pupil makes a given demonstration his own, it becomes his thought, he can use it in a new situation.
4. A pupil of himself demonstrates a proposition that has been proposed by another.
5. A pupil of himself sees in a situation the mathematical relations dominating it and of himself solves the problem he has thus abstracted from the gross situation.

Dr. Kilpatrick then takes the position that teachers should center their attention on this fifth possibility as "the next step in method." He states that "as teachers we are concerned not merely with the objective goals reached by the pupils, but quite as truly with the actual searchings themselves. The good teacher of mathematics nowadays knows, perhaps as do few others, that to have searched and found, leaves a pupil a different person from what he would be if he merely understands and accepts the results of others' search and formulation."

These quotations give explicit recognition to some of the implications of the three basic assumptions previously stated, and it is recognized that methods and processes consistent with these implications have far-reaching significance for classroom procedure. A careful and detailed description of the "methods and processes" used in this study will be given in the following chapter. While these data are of major im-

[7] W. H. Kilpatrick, "The Next Step in Method," *The Mathematics Teacher*, Vol. xv, No. 1, 1922, pp. 16–25.

portance from the standpoint of effective learning, it should also be recognized that they affect the nature of the content considered.

DATA DEALING WITH CONTENT

Since the student is to "have the opportunity to reason about the subject matter of geometry in his own way," no definite sequence of theorems can be arranged in advance. In *The Teaching of Geometry in Schools*,[8] a report prepared for the Mathematical Association of Great Britain, there is the following significant statement: "The Committee is convinced that it is neither desirable nor possible to insist that one sequence shall be imposed on all teachers and all pupils. But for a definite pupil a definite sequence is needed." While the writer accepts the general principle expressed in this statement, he does not interpret it as meaning that there is one and only one sequence which will most effectively meet the needs of any given pupil. The sequence for an individual pupil will vary with the environment, and it should not be overlooked that the teacher is a factor in this environment. He is acquainted with the domain which the pupil is about to enter, and it is his responsibility as guide and counsellor to assist the pupil in developing whatever sequence will give him the greatest sense of accomplishment. What particular theorems are covered is not a matter of great concern, since the emphasis is to be placed on the nature of the process by which these theorems are proved and not on the theorems themselves.

There is also considerable variation in the number of theorems which should be covered in any individual case. Since the major purpose of this experience is to give pupils an understanding of the nature of proof, is any particular purpose served by further study of geometric theorems once this result has been achieved? Furthermore, does this not imply a careful program of evaluation if a teacher is to know when the law of diminishing returns begins to operate?

Mr. Henry Shanholt raises the same question in the following vigorous language: "I am concerned with this 'one

[8] Mathematical Association Report, *The Teaching of Geometry in Schools*, p. 19–20. G. Bell and Sons, Ltd., London, 1929.

year' idea. If we wish our pupils to acquire the ability to understand the need of a formal logical proof, to develop powers and habits of careful, accurate and independent think-ing . . . what foundation have we from which to assume that he will have reached the optimum ability at the end of one year? What scientific basis is there for the constant pounding of the inductive-deductive method of reasoning, day in and day out for the extent of one year?"[9] While this is a very pertinent question and one which must be answered, there are students who derive such genuine satisfaction from proving theorems which they, themselves, have discovered through thinking about the subject matter of geometry in their own way that they wish to prolong this type of experi-ence. Furthermore, there is much of educational value in group consideration and critical analysis of theorems dis-covered by individual pupils, and by means of such discus-sions the results achieved by one pupil often tend to influence the accomplishment of others.

While one purpose of this study is to suggest classroom procedures whereby the student will have the opportunity "to think about the subject matter of geometry in his own way" and to have a part in guiding the development of the work, another purpose is to discover just what sort of content such procedures will yield. If a teacher is sensitive to the "children's logic" what concepts will remain undefined? To what extent will the vocabulary of geometry be developed and how will definitions be stated? What assumptions will be made and to what extent will the implications of these assumptions be discovered? Answers to these questions for the twenty-five students in the experimental group already described will be given in Chapter IV and these answers will constitute data which are geometric in character.

In view of the way in which transfer is effected it is essen-tial to develop this material "in connection with the field to which transfer is desired." The Third Committee on Geom-etry[10] has something to say on this point. When asked how

[9] Henry H. Shanholt, "A New Deal in Geometry," *The Mathematics Teacher,* Vol. xxix, No. 2, 1936, pp. 67–68.

[10] Ralph Beatley, "Third Report of the Committee on Geometry," *The Mathe-matics Teacher,* Vol. xxviii, No. 7, 1935, p. 449.

teachers of geometry should modify their ordinary methods of teaching in order "to secure the transfer of those broader attitudes and appreciations which are commonly said to be most easily transferable," the members of this committee gave such answers as the following:

"Bring logical method to the forefront of consciousness; teach for transfer."

"Consciously teach the things we want."

"Actually do transferring from geometry to other fields."

"Apply forms of reasoning to non-mathematical situations."

"Point out the parallel between thinking in geometry and in other fields."

"Bring in illustrations to show the place of logical thinking in life."

"Pay more attention to originals and to analysis."

In this study, then, "the parallel between thinking in geometry and in other fields" will be pointed out and illustrations drawn from many fields of thought will be used "to show the place of logical thinking in life." It should be recognized, however, that the method of thought used in proving a geometric theorem is there applied to idealized concepts and the pupil should understand the limitations of this method in more complex "life situations." He will be encouraged to suggest situations wherein he has recognized the possibility of transfer. Another purpose of this study is to discover the kind of non-mathematical material to which pupils have found this method of thought applicable.

In the "Third Report of the Committee on Geometry" Mr. Joseph McCormack is quoted as saying, "I would like to see a fairly large number of schools try consciously to carry over geometry to life situations by asking questions on non-geometric material and attempting to get the pupils to apply their geometric types of reasoning to these problems. Perhaps a good collection of life situations could be worked out to which geometric reasoning could be applied with a minimum of tacit assumptions. A question on College Entrance or Regents examinations on this sort of thing, at first optional and later required, would stimulate a more active attempt at transfer."[11] While one might question the advisability of

[11] Ralph Beatley, *op. cit.*, p. 343.

"a minimum of tacit assumptions," it is possible that the material used in this study, a large part of which was suggested by the students in the experimental group, may constitute such a "collection." It will be outlined in the following chapter and will constitute data which are non-mathematical in character.

SUMMARY

The two types of data which are of major importance in this study are:

1. Methods and processes which make it possible for the student "to reason about the subject matter of geometry in his own way."
2. The content which is an outgrowth of the student's thinking.
   a. The geometric material.
   b. The non-geometric material to which "transfer" has been made.

Of the five independent experimental programs suggested by the Committee on Geometry this program most closely resembles *Va*, which makes "provision of 'transfer' material to facilitate application of the logical discipline of demonstrative geometry and the appreciation of its logical structure to non-geometric situations in real life."[12] Of the twenty-one committee members who ranked these experimental programs in order of promise, thirteen placed *Va* first, one placed it second, two placed it fourth, one placed it fifth, while four failed to record their opinion. In the same report Professor Upton is quoted as saying, "As to experiments I consider *Va* outstandingly most promising and worth while. I know of nothing else that I should put ahead of it."[13] In Chapter V of the present study an evaluation of the results of such a program will be given.

[12] Ralph Beatley, *op. cit.*, p. 340.
[13] *Ibid.*, p. 343.

CHAPTER III

A DESCRIPTION OF PROCEDURES

IT WAS the purpose of the writer to have an individual conference with each of the twenty-five pupils in the experimental group before the opening of school. It was not possible to arrange all these conferences and when the class met for its first session there were still eleven pupils with whom the teacher had not had an opportunity to confer. The conferences were arranged during the first week of school and there is little reason to believe that the few class sessions held in the meantime had any marked effect on the pupil's attitude. Through these conferences the teacher hoped to secure some understanding of each pupil's attitude toward mathematics in general and toward demonstrative geometry in particular.

The conference was most informal in character. No questionnaire was given to the pupil and no notes were taken during the interview. The teacher tried to make the pupil feel that he was definitely interested in helping him and that this help could be most effective only when the teacher understood the true nature of the pupil's attitude toward the work he was about to begin. The pupil was encouraged to talk freely and little direction was given to the conversation by the teacher until he felt that such an attempt to guide the discussion would not destroy the pupil's confidence in the situation. In the judgment of the teacher, there were only three instances where the pupil failed to talk honestly and frankly concerning himself and his attitude toward mathematics.

Immediately following the interview, the teacher made careful note of the pupil's comments which, in his opinion, gave indication of the pupil's attitude toward geometry. Although there was great variation in the form of these comments they fall into the general classification given in Table 5. This table also indicates the number of pupils in each

TABLE 5

COMMENTS REVEALING ATTITUDE OF PUPILS TOWARD
THE STUDY OF DEMONSTRATIVE GEOMETRY

Kind of Comment Made by Pupils	Number Making Comment
If this work were not required I would not take it.	19
I need it to go to college.	18
I like the faculty. Since they require this course there must be some value in it.	12
I have heard that geometry is very difficult and I know I will not be able to do it.	10
Why should I know any more geometry? What I know already is of no use to me.	9
I have had enough geometry. I don't need any more.	8
I don't see any value in memorizing a lot of things which I will never use.	8
I have to take something and this will probably be as good as anything else.	3
I need geometry for later work which I want to take.	3
What does "demonstrative" mean?	2
I know I shall like geometry for I have always liked mathematics.	2

classification. There is, of course, a considerable amount of overlapping.

While one should be cautious in drawing any generalizations from these data, it is clear that at least nineteen of the twenty-five pupils were taking the work only because it was required. This is doubtless true also of the three who thought it would "probably be as good as anything else." Most of the pupils who had had any work in informal geometry considered it as a continuation of that sort of experience, and only two of them raised any questions as to the significance of the word "demonstrative." In general, it is probably safe to say that twenty-two of the twenty-five pupils had a negative attitude toward studying any more mathematics, although twelve of the twenty-two thought "there must be some value in it," otherwise the faculty would not require it. They "liked" the faculty and because of this apparently had some faith in their judgment.

RECOGNITION OF NEED FOR DEFINITION

As the first step in leading the pupils to understand something of "the nature of proof," it seemed important that they should recognize the necessity for clarity of definition in all matters where precise thinking is essential. To understand how the vagueness and ambiguity of ordinary words lead to serious errors in reflective thought is to appreciate the importance of clearly defined concepts in any technical vocabulary. It seemed advisable, then, to begin this work with a consideration of the importance of definition in matters which claimed the interest of the pupils, and the teacher gave careful thought as to what illustrations would be most helpful for this purpose. He recalled that during the preceding school year there had been a good deal of animated discussion concerning awards and that the question of whether or not awards were to be made for "outstanding achievements" in the school was still unsettled. Here, then, was a problem of real significance to the pupils about which there had been some controversy and in the consideration of which definition was likely to be an important issue. The teacher decided to give them an opportunity to discuss this problem, anticipating that in the argument which was almost certain to develop the necessity for clarity of definition would be recognized.

When the class met for the first time most of the pupils had their notebooks with them, some of the more thoughtful had brought their compasses and straightedges, and all of them expected to be given a text from which the work of the year would be taken.

There was thus considerable surprise when, after the usual routine of the opening day had been completed, the teacher said, "There is no great hurry about beginning our regular work in geometry and since the problem of awards is one which is soon to be considered by the entire school body I suggest that we give some preliminary consideration to the proposition that 'awards should be granted for outstanding achievement in the school'." While it developed that within this particular group there were not many pupils who openly opposed the granting of awards, the opposition that was offered was thoughtful and intelligent.

Within a very few moments after the discussion started the question was raised as to whether a teacher's salary was an award. One pupil argued that everybody worked for an award of some kind. Another asked whether playing on the football team constituted an "outstanding achievement" while another believed that grades on academic achievement were awards. Vigorous disagreement developed, even among those who were supporting the general proposition that awards should be granted, and considerable time was spent in what might appear to have been useless discussion. However, when the teacher summarized the discussion, pointing out the differences that had developed and clarifying the real issues which had arisen one pupil said, "Most of this trouble is caused by the fact that we don't know what we mean by 'awards' or by 'outstanding achievement'"; and the evident agreement with this statement by other members of the class indicated that although the word "definition" was not used many of the pupils recognized in this situation the need for clearly defining these two ideas. The school body later decided to grant awards under certain conditions and one of the conditions was that the pupil receiving the award "must be a good citizen." In discussing this, one of the pupils promptly pointed out that before this award plan could be effectively administered "someone will have to explain what is meant by 'good citizen'."

In general, however, this explicit recognition of the need for definition seemed foreign to the thinking of the pupils. They were unable to select with any degree of accuracy the key words which need to be clearly defined before the real meaning of the statement in which they occur is evident. All of them agreed with the truth of the statement that "Abraham Lincoln spent very little time in school" and no one raised the point that the truth of this statement depends on how "school" is defined. However, when each pupil was asked to write his definition of "school" the results indicated that:

12 students considered "school" as a "building" set aside for certain purposes.

10 students considered "school" as a "place for learning things."

3 pupils considered "school" as "any experience from which one learns."

Before there was any discussion of the significance of these definitions the students were given the following short exercise:

Accepting the definition of "school" as "Any experience from which one learns" indicate your agreement or disagreement with the proposition:

"Abraham Lincoln spent very little time in school."

One pupil was absent when this exercise was considered, but of the twenty-four present all of them now disagreed with this proposition. A comparison of these results with those previously obtained from the same pupils served to emphasize the importance of definition and illustrated how a changed definition does affect conclusions. The teacher also used this opportunity to point out that when two people are discussing "school," and one of them defines it as a "building" while the other defines it as "any experience from which one learns," there is almost certain to be disagreement since the concept of "school" does not mean the same thing to each person.

Through such considerations the pupils began to recognize the need for clarity of definition, and as this recognition developed they began to suggest illustrations which were interesting to them. Among these were such points as the following:

1. Is the librarian a teacher?
2. What is an aristocrat?
3. What is one hundred percent Americanism?
4. How do I know when I am tardy?
5. What is a "safety" in football?
6. What is a "foul ball" in baseball?
7. What is the labor class?
8. What is an obscene book?

These suggestions, together with the many others that were made, not only reflect the interests of the pupils but also suggest how concepts and ideas can be developed "in connection with the field to which transfer is desired." While it was neither possible nor advisable to give detailed consideration to all of these points, numbers 4, 5 and 6 seemed to the teacher to have possibilities which should not be overlooked. Each pupil was familiar with the fact that when tardy for any class he could not be admitted without an "admit slip" which he secured at the office. One pupil made the point that he was considered tardy for one class and not for another, although the circumstances were the same. The teacher pointed out that the respective teachers involved had different definitions of "tardy." He then suggested that the pupils define "tardy" for that particular class and after some discussion, to which the teacher contributed as well as the pupils, they defined a pupil as tardy "when he reached the classroom after the door was closed." The teacher then pointed out that each time a pupil met the requirements of this definition, the rule concerning admittance to the classroom implied certain conclusions as to what that pupil should do, and this served to illustrate something of the nature of implication.

A consideration of "safety" and "foul ball" brought an eager response from the pupils. They quickly pointed out that in baseball a "foul ball" had been defined, and it was the responsibility of the umpire to determine whether or not a ball which had been struck satisfied this definition. Similarly a pitched ball is a strike only when in the judgment of the umpire it meets the requirements of the definition of a strike. This whole question of games proved to be a most fruitful field, for in addition to the excellent illustrations of the importance of definition the rules served to illustrate the importance of agreements among people and how these agreements determined conclusions. No difficulty was met in leading the pupils to recognize that these rules were nothing more than agreements which a group of interested people had made and that they implied certain conclusions relative to the activities of the players.

When the question was raised as to what was the effect of changing one of these agreements, numerous pupils were ready to point out that the activities of the players were changed. Many illustrations were offered. One pupil explained how a new rule concerning the forward pass in football had changed the game in certain respects, while another discussed how the game of handball had been improved through a change in one of the rules on which the game was based. The teacher used such illustrations as these to introduce the pupil to the idea that conclusions usually depend on a set of rules to which people have agreed, or which they accept. These agreements may well be called assumptions and through numerous illustrations the pupil learns that even the most elementary activities of life depend on certain assumptions. The teacher of algebra assumes that his students understand arithmetic, the man who deposits his money in a bank assumes that the bank will not fail, the patient assumes that his doctor can cure him.

It is important to recognize that in this introduction the thinking of the pupils was concerned with situations which were interesting and familiar to them. Most of the illustrations used were suggested by the pupils and reflected their interests. However, it was the responsibility of the teacher to guide the discussion in such a way that the attention of the pupils was focussed on the important principles, common to all illustrations, and not on the illustrations themselves. He suggested that these principles be made explicit and after considerable discussion the following summary was made:

1. Definition is helpful in all cases where precise thinking is to be done.
2. Conclusions seem to depend on assumptions but often the assumptions are not recognized.
3. It is difficult to agree on definitions and assumptions in situations which cause one to become excited.

It should be pointed out that this summary is not the work of the teacher alone. It represents the joint thinking of the teacher and pupils. The statements when originally made were not in this form. They were awkwardly expressed and the ideas were none too clear. Some pupils objected to these original statements and suggested improvements. The teacher felt free to contribute in the same manner as other members of the group, and it was through such discussion and joint thinking that the original statements were refined and ultimately accepted, as expressed above, by all pupils.

INTRODUCTION TO SPACE CONCEPTS, UNDEFINED TERMS, DEFINITIONS AND ASSUMPTIONS

Following this introduction, which with this particular group required approximately four weeks, the thinking of the pupils was definitely guided to a consideration of space where the "ideas studied are devoid of strong emotional content"

and "the pupils' native ability to think is not stifled by prejudice or bias." The pupils had already realized that "it is
difficult to agree on definitions and assumptions in situations
which cause one to become excited" and to illustrate this it
was only necessary to remind them of the vigorous controversy which developed in our attempt to define "aristocrat"
and "labor class." There was general agreement that it
would be interesting to make definitions and assumptions
about concepts which did not stir the emotions and to proceed to investigate their implications. Many suggestions
were made as to the content with which these definitions and
assumptions would deal. Some pupils suggested "government," some suggested "religion," while others suggested
"war." All of these suggestions were rejected by the group
since they did not satisfy the criterion that the concepts involved should be "devoid of strong emotional content."
The fact is that no suggestions were offered which did satisfy
this criterion until the teacher raised the question whether or
not one was likely to "become excited" in thinking about
space. This question apparently reminded the pupils that
they had originally expected to study geometry, and the discussion which followed resulted in an agreement to "build a
theory about the space in which we live."

There was no question about the interest of the pupils. All
of them had participated in the discussion to some degree and
all were anxious to begin to "build" this theory. However,
there was some difficulty in knowing just how to begin. Their
background had led them to believe that they should begin
by agreeing on certain definitions, but there was no agreement as to what should be defined. One pupil said that space
involved "great distances," and that perhaps "We should
begin by defining distance." Another said that he could "fill
up the space in the room with cubes," and he thought it would
be well to begin by defining "cube." This suggestion received feeble support. Another suggested, however, that he
could "fill up the space in the room by piling a lot of flat sur-
faces one on top of the other and so we might just as well
begin by defining 'surface' as 'cube'." This suggestion also
received feeble support. Another said he would like to begin
by defining "triangle" for he knew that "triangles had some-

thing to do with geometry." Someone else suggested that "squares also had something to do with geometry" and that "we might begin by defining them." A large majority of the pupils made no suggestions whatever, although some of them supported either the "cube" or the "surface."

The teacher wrote on the board all the suggestions that had been made and asked the pupils to select one of these concepts and define it. No one attempted to define "cube" or "surface" although these were the only suggestions that received any support when made. Two pupils attempted to define "distance," while the remainder selected either "triangle" or "square." From the discussion which followed it was evident that degree of familiarity with the concept was the basis of selection rather than anything else. The teacher examined these definitions carefully and selected for discussion at the next meeting of the class those which he considered typical. These were written on the board. They varied widely in meaning and precision of statement, and the pupils were asked to suggest any improvements they thought desirable. Comparatively few responded and the suggestions that were offered had no particular significance. The general inability of these pupils to recognize looseness of expression was particularly noticeable. After some discussion which resulted in minor improvements, the pupils were willing to accept each of the three definitions which follow:

A *triangle* is a figure with three lines as sides.

A *square* is a figure having four sides of the same length and four right angles.

The *distance* between two points is the length of the line joining them.

The teacher pointed out that acceptance of these definitions really implied that the words used in them had the same meaning for each of the pupils. Attention was thus directed to a consideration of these words and the question was raised as to what is meant by "figure," "line," "side," "angle," "point" and "length," these being the only words questioned. In the course of the discussion which followed one pupil said, "Everyone knows what a line is," and when another pupil asked whether he meant "straight line" or "curved line" he replied that "It made no difference for everyone knows what a straight line is and everyone knows what a curved line is." The teacher considered this to be a most important statement and wanted the class to appreciate its significance. He asked whether they agreed with this pupil. Is the concept of "straight line" the same in the thinking of all people? Does everyone know "what a straight line is"? Do people in Moscow, Rome, Paris and Berlin have the same concept of "straight line" as the people in Columbus? All the pupils agreed that "straight line" did mean the same thing to all people and that no useful purpose would be served in attempting to define it.

Here then was a concept concerning the meaning of which there was apparently no vagueness or ambiguity *in the minds of the pupils*. It was accepted as meaning the same thing to all of them, and the question was raised as to whether the other significant words in the three accepted definitions were of the same nature. Each of them was carefully considered and after some discussion the pupils agreed to accept "point" and "angle" as concepts which were unambiguous and without vagueness. There was disagreement concerning "figure," "side" and "length," which raised some doubt whether the original definitions should now be accepted. However, no attempt was made to revise them at that time for it seemed evident to the teacher that the thinking of the pupils had turned in a direction which offered more promising results. Some of them recognized at once that instead of beginning the study of space by defining certain concepts it was much better and, in fact, necessary to begin with the selection of a few concepts about the meaning of which there was no disagreement and for which explicit definition was unnecessary. While the real significance of this was not recognized at that time by all pupils, the importance of and the necessity for these "primitive concepts" became increasingly clear to them as the work developed.

Up to this time there had been no general consideration of a textbook. While some pupils had wanted to know "What text is to be used," it was now generally recognized by all of them that to use any text would spoil to a large extent the opportunity for the kind of thinking they had been doing. Each pupil was thus encouraged to develop his own text and was given freedom to develop it in his own way. This procedure is consistent with the assumptions in the preceding chapter, for while group discussions usually resulted in common agreement concerning the undefined terms, the definitions and assumptions, each pupil was given opportunity to express his own individuality in organization, in arrangement, in clarity of presentation and in the kind and number of implications established. Most of the pupils called this text "A Theory of Space" and they now recognized that to build this theory it was essential to select a few concepts which were without ambiguity and which meant the same to all of them. They decided to call these "The Undefined Terms" and the first section of the text was to be used for the purpose of listing these terms as they were agreed to in the development of the work. This list began with "point," "straight line" and "angle," which had already been accepted. The teacher, however, reminded the pupils that they had agreed to build a theory of space and the question was raised as to whether or not these three primitive concepts belonged in the construction of such a theory. Had "point," "straight line" and "angle" any relation to space? In answer to this one pupil said, "I think space is full of points," and through questions and suggestions from both teacher and pupils the following agreements were reached:

There are points in space.

A line can be drawn through any two points.

These were recognized as assumptions and it is important to observe that they were made *by the pupils* and considered *by them* to have originated in their own thinking.

To illustrate the second of these assumptions the teacher placed two points on the board and asked any pupils who felt they could draw a line through these two points to volunteer for this purpose. One was selected from the large number responding and he drew a straight line through the two points. The teacher then asked another pupil to draw the line he had in mind and he said it would be "the same line." Other pupils who had volunteered were invited to "draw a line through these two points," but the general reply was that "the line had already been drawn." Now there is a big difference between "a line" and "the line." This difference was emphasized by the teacher, who then drew a curved line through these same two points. Immediately the pupils said that they meant "a straight line" and that there was "only one such line" through these two points. The suggestion was made that "line" should always mean "straight line" and he assumption was then revised by the pupils to read "One and only one line can be drawn through any two points."

The teacher asked the pupils how long this line was. Some of them replied that its length was determined by "the distance between the two points," while others said that it was just "as long as you want to make it." This led to considerable discussion out of which grew the idea that "a line could be extended in either direction just as far as you want to extend it," and this was finally accepted by all pupils as a third assumption. No pupil recognized that certain properties of space were implicit in this assumption, and when the teacher raised this question one pupil did point out that "we are assuming that space has no end." With one or two exceptions, however, this point had at that time no significance to the pupils. The assumption seemed reasonable to them and was validated by their own experience.

The discussion which led to the preceding assumption also focussed the attention of the pupils on the portion of the line between the two points. They referred to this as "a piece of the line," and pointed out that the length of this "piece" was the distance between the two points. The concept of "line segment" was thus introduced, and the pupils made the following definitions:

A *line segment* is a piece of a line.

The *length of a line segment* is the distance between its two end points.

Considerable emphasis was given to the fact that these two concepts, "line segment" and "length of a line segment," were defined in terms of other concepts which were undefined. When asked what these undefined concepts were the pupils replied that they were "point" and "line." No question whatever was raised concerning "distance," although this was one of the concepts for which definition was earlier attempted. It is significant that later on when the thinking of the pupils was more critical both "distance" and "between" were selected as terms which needed defining. However, after an effort was made to define them they were placed among the undefined terms.

As an exercise which offered promising possibilities the following suggestions were given the students:

> On a piece of paper locate any two points, A and B, and draw the line AB. Then locate two different points, X and Y. What are all possible relations which line AB can have to line XY? Considering *only* lines AB and XY, write down all the properties of the resulting figure which you either know or are willing to accept.

Different pupils expressed "all possible relations" of these two lines in very different language. The relations which they tried to express are given in Table 6, which also indicates the number of pupils recognizing the possibility of each kind of relation.

TABLE 6

POSSIBLE RELATIONS BETWEEN ANY TWO LINES RECOGNIZED BY THE PUPILS

Relations Recognized by the Pupils	Number Recognizing Relation
Intersecting lines	25
Parallel lines	11
Perpendicular lines	9
Skew lines	3

The properties of the figure either "known" or "accepted" were also expressed in a variety of ways. However, on analyzing the statements it was clear that the following points had been made:

> Lines AB and CD can be extended indefinitely in either direction.
>
> When two lines intersect four angles are formed.
>
> Vertical angles are equal.
>
> The sum of the angles about a point is 360°.
>
> If the lines are perpendicular each of the four angles is 90°.
>
> A straight angle contains 180°.
>
> Parallel lines will never meet.
>
> Skew lines are not in the same plane.
>
> Two lines intersect in a point.

These results reflect the retention of ideas to which some of the pupils had been introduced in a study of informal geometry. However, although they showed some familiarity with the facts, there was evident need for a clarification of the concepts. The statements of the pupils were classified and samples were selected for criticism by the entire class. These were written on the board and as a result of the general discussion which followed "plane" and "equal" were added to the list of undefined terms, definitions were written for the following concepts:

> vertical angles
> right angle
> straight angle
> intersecting lines
> perpendicular lines
> parallel lines
> skew lines

while there was general agreement that the following statements should be accepted as assumptions:

> Vertical angles are equal.
> Two lines can intersect at one and only one point.
> One and only one plane can be passed through two intersecting lines.
> One and only one plane can be passed through two parallel lines.
> One and only one plane can be passed through a line and a point not on the line.
> One and only one plane can be passed through three points which are not in the same line.

When the pupils later became familiar with the idea that certain factors "determine" certain other factors and when they understood the full significance of this concept, they revised the preceding five assumptions to read as follows:

> Two intersecting lines determine one and only one point.
> Two intersecting lines determine one and only one plane.
> Two parallel lines determine one and only one plane.
> A line and a point not on the line determine one and only one plane.
> Three non-collinear points determine one and only one plane.

The word "collinear" had been accepted to replace "in the same line," while "non-collinear" had been accepted to mean "not in the same line." Similarly, the word "coplanar" was accepted to mean "in the same plane."

It is well, at this point, to make explicit certain procedures which are illustrated in the preceding discussion and which have a strong influence on the content.

1. *With respect to the undefined terms.*

   a. The terms that were to remain undefined were selected and accepted by the pupils as clear and unambiguous.

   b. No attempt was made to reduce the number of undefined terms to a minimum.

2. *With respect to the definitions.*

   a. The need for each definition was recognized by the pupils through discussion. Definitions were an outgrowth of the work rather than the basis for it.

   b. Definitions were made by the pupils. Loose and ambiguous statements were refined and improved by criticisms and suggestions until they were tentatively accepted by all pupils.

3. *With respect to the assumptions.*

   a. Propositions which seemed obvious to the pupils were accepted as assumptions when needed.

   b. These assumptions were made explicit by the pupils and were considered by them as the product of their own thinking.

   c. No attempt was made to reduce the number of assumptions to a minimum.

   d. The detection of implicit or tacit assumptions was encouraged and recognized as important.

   e. The pupils recognized that, at best, the formal list of assumptions is incomplete.

In addition to the section for "the undefined terms," each pupil reserved in his text a section for "definitions" and recorded in this section all definitions made in the development of the theory. Similarly, another section was reserved for listing the "assumptions" and new assumptions were added to the list as the need for them was recognized.

While "angle" was accepted as one of the undefined terms, the teacher suggested that the pupils think of an angle as being generated by the rotation of a line about a fixed point in a fixed line. This was illustrated by using the hands of a clock and many additional illustrations were given by the pupils, such as a pair of compasses, a pair of scissors and the like. The concept of angle was thus enlarged to include "amount of rotation," and in developing this idea it was pointed out that the rotation might be in either a clockwise or a counter-clockwise direction from the given fixed line. While the pupils felt that they should agree as to the direction of rotation, they also felt that this was a point of minor importance. One pupil pointed out that this situation resembled the number scale to some extent, since from any given point on the number scale one could go "either in the positive or negative direction." This was an important contribution to the group thinking, and by emphasizing the resemblance suggested it soon became apparent to the pupils that if the rotation in one direction is considered as generating a positive angle the rotation in the other direction may be considered as generating a negative angle. The pupils were unanimous in believing that the angle should be positive when the rotation was clockwise and negative when it was counter-clockwise. They were surprised to learn that mathematicians had agreed to consider counter-clockwise as generating a positive angle, but accepted this convention "since it is not important anyway."

As an outgrowth of the preceding discussion "fixed" and "rotation" were added to the list of undefined terms, while the following concepts were defined:

vertex	obtuse angle
initial side	reflex angle
terminal side	adjacent angles
acute angle	

Perhaps it should again be emphasized that definitions were made by the pupils *after* a recognition of the characteristics of the concept to be defined. For example, the definition of adjacent angles was an outgrowth of the discussion which resulted from a consideration of the following points:

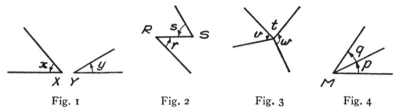

| Fig. 1 | Fig. 2 | Fig. 3 | Fig. 4 |

In Figure 1, what is the vertex of angle x? What is the vertex of angle y? What is the initial side of angle x? What is the terminal side? What is the initial side of angle y and what is the terminal side? Do these angles have any elements in common? If so, what are they? The angles in each of the other diagrams were examined in a similar manner and such an examination served to emphasize the characteristics of angles p and q which make the relation between these angles uniquely different from the relation between the two angles in each of the other diagrams. When the contributions of the pupils were of such a character as to indicate that they recognized these characteristics, the teacher told them that the name given to angles thus related was "adjacent angles." He then asked for a definition of adjacent angles and there was unanimous agreement that:

Adjacent angles are angles that have a common vertex and a common side.

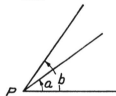

The teacher then drew angles a and b as in the accompanying figure and asked if they did not meet the requirements of this definition. He then asked if the relation between a and b was the same as the relation between angles p and q in Figure 4. There was an immediate response to this and all the pupils were ready to accept the corrected definition given by one of them:

Adjacent angles are angles that have a common vertex and a common side between them.

It is interesting to note that the pupils originally agreed that "An acute angle is one which is less than 90°." Later, however, it was pointed out by one of the pupils that "According to that definition −30° is an acute angle." No one disagreed with that statement, but when another pupil asked if −100° was an acute angle it became clear that the original definition included angles which were not meant to be included. After some discussion it was changed to read, "An acute angle is an angle which is greater than 0° and less than 90°."

The teacher frequently reminded the pupils that they were building "A Theory of Space" and that wherever possible their thinking should extend beyond the plane into three dimensions. Reminders of this nature soon became unnecessary, and many concepts of space were developed. The question was raised, for example, as to whether it was possible to rotate one plane about another plane just as a line could be rotated about another line. Through consideration of this problem, for which numerous illustrations were given, the concept of dihedral angles was developed, while the following assumptions were suggested and accepted by the pupils:

If two planes intersect, they can intersect in one and only one line.

Vertical dihedral angles are equal.

The teacher discouraged any attempt by the pupils to memorize the definitions and assumptions accepted. On the other hand, each pupil was encouraged to use his text freely and to refer to whatever definitions and assumptions he needed in the development of his work. This served to emphasize the importance of his text and was a strong factor in encouraging him to keep it neat, well organized and always up to date. As new definitions and assumptions were made they were written in the text with numerous illustrations and supplementary comments, depending on the interests and abilities of the individual pupils.

Misuse and loose interpretations of these basic concepts were unusually rare, largely, in the opinion of the writer, because of the fact that they were an outgrowth of the thinking of the pupils. When a term was used incorrectly, in either oral or written discussion, the pupil was referred to his text to check on his statement for the definition of that term. It was by such means and not by memorization that the pupils became familiar with the technical language they were helping to create.

DEFINITION IN NON-MATHEMATICAL SITUATIONS

The interest of the pupils was at all times particularly noticeable. They participated actively in discussion and there was increasing evidence that they were learning to think together. The emotional controversy which had marked earlier efforts to define "aristocrat" and "labor class" was noticeably lacking in their efforts to define mathematical concepts, and the teacher pointed out the desirability of thinking about the pressing problems of democracy in this same objective manner. To provide opportunity for this kind of activity exercises similar to the following were prepared and in many instances the content of such exercises was suggested by the pupils:

In the administration of certain Ohio Laws it became necessary to know just what a restaurant is, and in connection with this problem the following editorial appeared in one of the Columbus papers:

"What Is a Restaurant?"

"The art of precise definition is not so easy as it may seem. To produce an acceptable definition of a dog calls for ability in the art of lucid and exact statement. . . .

* * * * * * *

"What is a restaurant? Well, a harder order to fill would be: What is a drug store? To say it is a place where commerce in drugs is carried on is as far afield as to say restaurants are places where people can rest their aunts.

"Well, the Ohio State Restaurant Association has tackled the job, has drafted a definition and will ask the Ohio Legislature to give them the sanction of their approval when they say that a restaurant is a place of business where 50 per cent or more of the gross sales accrue from the sale of food-stuffs consumed on the premises."

Now, in view of the way in which "restaurant" has been defined by the Ohio State Restaurant Association, let us consider the following questions:

1. The major part of the gross sales of the Atlantic and Pacific Tea Company is of foodstuffs. Can these stores rightly be called restaurants? Why?

2. The gross sales of one of the White Castles in Columbus is approximately $12,000 a year, all of this coming from the sale of food. Some of this food is eaten where purchased while the remainder is eaten elsewhere. If the amount eaten elsewhere is $6,185.40, is the White Castle rightly called a restaurant?

3. In 1934 the gross sales of a business amounted to $18,439.27. These sales were distributed as follows: drugs, $9,203.12; ice cream, $3,297.65; candy, $1,069.60 and lunches, $4,868.90. In the light of these data discuss the problem as to whether this place of business is a restaurant.

4. How would you decide whether or not a combined ice cream parlor and soda fountain which also serves light lunches is a restaurant?

5. Discuss the problem as to whether or not a place which sells beer and liquor and also serves sandwiches as well as other types of food is a restaurant."

This proved to be a most profitable exercise. It stimulated thoughtful discussion, and the point was very definitely made that before this suggested definition could be effective in distinguishing restaurants from other places of business in Ohio, "foodstuffs," "consumed" and "on the premises" must also be carefully defined.

An amendment to the constitution of Ohio which removed the sales tax on "food" also presented an interesting illustration of the importance of definition and this situation is used in the following exercise.

On November 3 the voters of Ohio approved the constitutional amendment which provides that "on and after Nov. 11, 1936, no excise tax shall be collected upon the sale or purchase of food for human consumption off the premises where sold." What words in this amendment must be clearly defined in order to make effective the administration of the law?

A number of questions similar to those which are sure to arise any time after this law is put into effect are suggested below. Consider each of these questions and in view of the above amendment answer them in accordance with your best judgment. In each case point out the factors on which your answer depends:

1. Mr. Carter went into an A and P store and purchased three pounds of beef. He happened to say he was buying this meat for his dog and the clerk insisted that a tax be charged. Was the charge legal?

2. Mrs. Page purchased a bottle of cod liver oil at the drugstore. She expected to pay a tax on this purchase but the clerk told her that was unnecessary. Was the clerk correct in requiring no tax?

3. Fred wanted to buy a box of chocolates that was priced at $1.50. He had only $1.50 in his pocket and he hesitated to ask for the chocolates because he feared he would have to pay a tax on the purchase. Were his fears justified?

4. A twelve-year-old girl went to the store to buy some baking chocolate for her mother. The clerk charged her a tax on the purchase. When the mother learned of this she said the clerk had made an error. She telephoned him and asked that the tax be refunded. Do you think she should get this refund?

5. Mr. Smith asked his friend to dine with him at the Statler Hotel in Cleveland. He had this dinner served in his room on the tenth floor. Was the waiter justified in charging Mr. Smith a tax on the amount of his bill?

6. Joe lived on the tenth floor of an apartment house and bought his groceries from a store located on the first floor of the same apartment house. He argues that his groceries were consumed "off the premises" and that therefore they were not taxable. Do you agree with him?

7. Tom bought fifty cents worth of apples at a fruit store and paid no tax on them. However, when the fruit merchant saw Tom eating these apples while seated in his car which was parked directly in front of the fruit store he asked him for the tax. Should Tom pay it?

8. Discuss in general the difficulties which are likely to occur in administering this law. How can they be avoided?

For the purpose of further emphasizing the necessity of clearly defining "significant words and phrases" before the statements which contain them can have any real meaning, the educational planks in the state platforms of the Republican and Democratic parties of Ohio in the 1934 election were selected and the exercise which appears on page 49 was prepared:

This kind of exercise had a most helpful effect on the thinking of the pupils. To compare the way in which the governor might handle the educational problems of the state with the educational plank of the platform on which he was elected, deeply impressed the pupils with the real need for clear definitions of such terms as "adequate," "fair," "sufficient" and "proper" in all such documents.

Here are two statements relating to the education of the boys and girls of Ohio. Statement One represents A's viewpoint on this problem while Statement Two represents B's viewpoint. These statements have little meaning until certain significant words or phrases are defined. In your opinion, what are these words or phrases? List them on the lines below the statements:

A's Viewpoint	B's Viewpoint
1. The education of childhood and youth is a fundamental obligation of state government. Therefore, we pledge ourselves to provide, without further delay and with safeguards which will preserve local control, financial support of our public schools that will establish and maintain a reasonable minimum standard of education throughout the state, to the end that every boy and girl in Ohio may secure an elementary and high school education.	2. We pledge an adequate program of state revenues, to be distributed by the state to the elementary and high schools of Ohio, in sufficient amounts to make up the deficiency in local revenues as determined by a fair foundation program and based upon proper economy of operation, fair and adequate salaries, and the maximum amount of local self help. The schools of Ohio must be kept open. The constitution guarantees education to the children of this state. We cannot afford nor can we tolerate any backward step in the education of the citizens of the future.

Let us now consider the following assumptions:

   1. That A and B are candidates for governor of Ohio.
   2. That education is the only issue between them.
   3. That you favor a strong and effective program of public education.

Under these circumstances for which of the two candidates would you vote?

Another exercise which led to much thoughtful discussion and which again emphasized the far-reaching importance of definition follows:

Not many years ago the Supreme Court of the United States rendered a decision concerning the relationship of the state to the schools of the state. In a unanimous decision the court ruled that the state had power over all schools in respect to the following matters and that it was the responsibility of the state:

1. To require "that all children of proper age attend some school."
2. To require "that teachers shall be of good moral character and patriotic disposition."
3. To require "that certain studies plainly essential to good citizenship must be taught."
4. To require "that nothing be taught which is manifestly inimical to public welfare."

Now before the state of Ohio or any other state can meet its responsibility as outlined in this decision it is essential to know just exactly what the decision means. Its meaning depends on certain significant words or phrases which it contains and the extent to which any state government will control the schools of the state depends, among other things, on how it defines these words or phrases.

Read this decision carefully and thoughtfully. What, in your opinion, are the words and phrases which need careful definition in order to make the decision clear? List them in the space provided below:

_____

_____

_____

_____

_____

This Supreme Court decision applies to all of the forty-eight states and presents the powers and responsibilities which each state has concerning the schools of the state. Now the educational opportunities of some states are definitely superior to those of certain other states and if we assume that each state government is equally effective in meeting its responsibilities for educating the young people of the state how may these wide differences in educational opportunity be explained?

The interpretation of papers of state is also an excellent illustration of the fundamental importance of definition. A part of the New Deal program, for example, was held to be unconstitutional because of the definition given to "Interstate Commerce." An illustration of this, which was very meaningful to pupils, occurred in the administration of the State government of Ohio and the following exercise was built around this situation:

The constitution of Ohio imposes certain obligations on the governor as to just how he is to handle a bill presented to him for his signature after it has been passed by both houses of the general assembly. One section of the constitution, for example, reads as follows:

"If he does not approve this bill, he shall return it with his objections in writing to the house in which it originated, which shall enter the objections at large upon its journal, and may then reconsider the vote on its passage. If three-fifths of the members elected to that house vote to repass the bill, it shall be sent, with the objections of the governor, to the other house, which may also reconsider the vote on its passage.

"If a bill shall not be returned by the governor within ten days, Sundays excepted, after being presented to him, it shall become a law in like manner as if he had signed it, unless the general assembly by adjournment prevents its return; in which case, it shall become a law unless, within ten days after such adjournment, it shall be filed by him, with his objections in writing, in the office of the secretary of state."

The second general appropriation bill, commonly known as "the revised budget bill," originated in the senate. It was approved by both houses of the general assembly and the governor received it for his signature on January 28. While awaiting the action of the governor the legislators took a recess until February 25 with a definite obligation to reassemble on that date. The governor did not wish to sign the bill as it was presented to him and vetoed certain items to the extent of $3,002,734. Then on February 7, in view of the fact that the legislature was not in session, he filed this bill together with his objections in the office of the secretary of state. Because of this action the legislators, when they reassembled on February 25, were unable to act on the governor's vetoes.

Some people believe that the governor did not comply with the obligations imposed upon him in the section of the constitution quoted above and therefore say that his vetoes are illegal. It is possible that this issue may be referred to the supreme court of Ohio for decision where it will be studied "without prejudice and in the clear light of logic." Considering the facts presented here:

"Do you believe that the governor handled this bill in accordance with the provisions of the constitution? What are the significant words in the constitution which must be defined before an opinion can be reached? How would you define these words?

"Present your analysis of this situation in logical form and state your decision as to the constitutionality of the way in which the governor handled this bill."

In their analysis of this situation most of the pupils were led to two different conclusions, depending on the way "recess" and "adjournment" were defined, and the exercise served to emphasize the great significance of definition in matters of far-reaching concern.

Exercises of this nature were not all given at one particular period. They were interspersed throughout the work of the year and were supplemented by thoughtful consideration of the points raised for discussion. The transfer value of this kind of exercise was almost immediately noticeable, for in other classes these pupils were asking that vagueness in the use of words be replaced by well defined terms, and they voluntarily contributed many illustrations[1] from other school experiences and from out-of-school situations wherein their own thinking had been clarified because of their improved ability to select "significant words and phrases" which needed definition before their meaning was clear.

IMPLICATIONS OF DEFINITIONS AND ASSUMPTIONS

At the beginning of one class session the teacher had drawn two intersecting lines on the board, as h and h' in the accompanying figure. Concerning this diagram he had written:

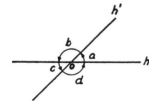

Assume that h is fixed in position and that h' revolves about O in a counterclockwise direction. State all the properties of the resulting figure that you are willing to accept.

While these "properties" were stated in a variety of ways the ideas were clear and, in general, well expressed. Two pupils were absent. The responses of the remaining twenty-three are summarized in Table 7.

[1] These illustrations have been summarized in Table 12, page 106.

TABLE 7

RELATIONS RECOGNIZED BY PUPILS WHEN ONE LINE
ROTATES ABOUT A FIXED POINT IN ANOTHER LINE

Response of Pupils	Number Making Response
h and *h'* can be extended indefinitely.	23
Vertical angles are always equal.	21
h and *h'* determine a plane.	23
Angles *a* and *c* get larger while angles *b* and *d* get smaller.	18
There is a time when the four angles formed are equal.	17
There is a time when *h* is perpendicular to *h'*.	15
When the four angles are equal *h* will be perpendicular to *h'*.	5
Angle *a* is never smaller than 0°.	3
Angle *a* is never larger than 360°.	3

These results were presented to the entire class. They were discussed, critically examined and clarified. One pupil pointed out that the last two were based on the assumption that *h'* started its rotation from the position of *h* and that its rotation was limited to one complete revolution. This discussion also led to the agreement that:

> If two lines intersect in such a manner that the adjacent angles thus formed are equal then the two lines are perpendicular.

Originally perpendicular lines had been defined as "two lines which make angles of 90° at their point of intersection," and the limitations of this definition were now apparent.

The properties of the accompanying diagram were similarly explored. In this case, the pupils were given the following suggestions:

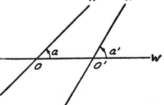

Assume that *w* and *h'* are two lines intersecting at *O'* and that *w* and *h'* are fixed in position. Let *O* be any point on *w* other than *O'* and let line *h* rotate about point *O*.

What properties of the resulting figure are you willing to accept?

While many of the properties listed resembled those in the preceding table, there were in addition other properties which related not only to the position of *h* with respect to *w* but also to the position of h with respect to h'. Attention was focussed on the three that follow:

There is a time when h is parallel to h'.
There is a time when angle a equals angle a'.
When angle a equals angle a' then h is parallel to h'.

While these properties were not listed by all the pupils, the last being given by two pupils only, they were accepted without objection and some pupils expressed annoyance that they had overlooked them. The teacher now referred to the original definition of parallel lines, which was "Parallel lines are lines that will never meet even though extended indefinitely in either direction," and pointed out that it would be difficult to show that two lines met the requirements of this definition just as it was impossible to show that two lines made angles of 90° at their point of intersection, since measurement is not permitted in demonstrative geometry. He further suggested that since perpendicular lines had now been defined in terms of "equal adjacent angles" it might be possible to define parallel lines in terms of equal angles. The response was prompt and one pupil gave the following definition:

Parallel lines are lines that have the same rotation from another line.

This definition was criticized and was soon corrected to read:

Parallel lines are lines that have the same amount of rotation from a line which intersects them.

The pupils now seemed willing to accept this definition and the teacher apparently agreed also. He then proceeded to draw different diagrams, inserting numerical values for the

sizes of the angles, and asked if the conditions were such as to make the lines parallel. Among these diagrams was one similar to the figure at the left and the usual question was asked, "Under the assumed conditions, is h parallel to h'?" This development served to make explicit that which the pupils had been assuming and illustrated most effectively the importance of "tacit assumptions." Many pupils then volunteered to correct further the definition of parallel lines and in its final form it was:

> Parallel lines are lines which have the same amount and direction of rotation from a line which intersects them.

Some question was raised as to the necessity for defining "direction," but there was general agreement that this concept belonged among the undefined terms.

Many of the implications of this definition were recognized at once. The teacher placed the accompanying diagram on the board and asked the pupils to assume that h and h' were parallel and that angle a equaled 80°. Without any apparent difficulty *all* pupils then gave correctly the size of each of the other angles in the figure. 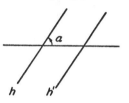 Later the problem was made more general and the pupils were asked to study the properties of the figure below in which h and h' are assumed to be parallel. No one failed to recognize that under these conditions $x = v$ and $w = v$. However, more than half the pupils limited their analysis to these two statements because (it was later learned) it was assumed, since only these angles were marked, that no others were to be considered. The other pupils, however, inserted additional letters and gave most of the familiar relations between the angles formed when two parallel 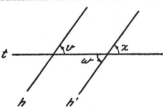 lines are cut by a transversal. These relations, however, were stated in terms of the particular angles in this diagram, and when the teacher suggested that they be generalized to cover all parallel lines the struggle to state these relations in general terms was found to be due to the difficulty of explaining just what angles were meant. For example, one pupil, in attempting to generalize the statement that $x = v$, expressed himself as follows:

> When two parallel lines are intersected by another line any outside angle is equal to the non-adjacent inside angle.

and when another pupil pointed out that "non-adjacent inside angle" might mean any one of the three "inside" angles that were non-adjacent to x, he revised his original statement as follows:

> When two parallel lines are intersected by another line any outside angle is equal to the non-adjacent inside angle on the same side of the line which intersects the two parallels.

The pupils recognized the awkwardness of such a statement and were ready for the suggestion of the teacher that a name be given to "the line which intersects the two parallels" and to any two angles so located with respect to this line as are angles x and v. As an outgrowth of this discussion the following definitions were accepted:

> A *transversal* is a line which intersects two or more other lines.
> When two lines are cut by a transversal any outside angle and the non-adjacent inside angle on the same side of the transversal are *corresponding angles*.

Before accepting this second definition, however, the question was raised as to how "outside" and "inside" were defined. After some discussion it was decided to place these among the undefined terms. The brevity and conciseness with which it was now possible to state the familiar theorem concerning "corresponding angles of parallel lines" impressed the pupils with the convenience of carefully defined terms. The idea of "converse statements" also developed from this discussion, and the point was made that when one accepts a definition he also accepts that definition when turned around. This was finally stated as "A definition when turned around is acceptable authority" and was regarded as an assumption.

Through a continuation of such processes the theorem concerning alternate interior angles of parallel lines was established and the class extended this to cover alternate exterior angles as well. Some of the pupils felt that these relations should be accepted as assumptions because "anyone can see those angles are equal," while others worked out deductive proofs for them because they "enjoyed it." Of the twenty-five pupils, however, no one suggested the relation between the two interior angles on the same side of the transversal, and the teacher directed their attention to this relation in the following manner:

Assume: h and h' to be two parallel lines cut by the transversal t.

Do these conditions imply any relation between angles a and c?

In their study of this situation some pupils gave a definite value to the size of angle a and then proceeded to show that for that particular value angles a and c were supplementary. They were encouraged to give other values to a and to see if the same relation held between a and c. Other pupils discovered this relation without using angles of definite size and presented a satisfactory proof for their conclusion. Five pupils made very little progress in the study of this figure until such questions were asked as "What is the sum of angles a and a'?" and "Do you know anything about angles a' and c?" Finally, both approaches to the proof of this theorem were discussed and examined. While the words "inductive" and "deductive" were not used, the essential difference between the two types of proof was emphasized and all pupils felt that the "deductive proof" was more convincing. It was pointed out, however, that this proof depended on an assumption which had not been stated explicitly and this led to an acceptance of the assumption that:

A quantity or magnitude may be substituted for its equal.

The first statement of this assumption was awkward, loose and inaccurate. This statement was criticized, improved and finally accepted as above expressed. However, in the course of this discussion numerous pupils asked how "quantity" and "magnitude" were defined and in the end these were placed among the undefined terms. The teacher then asked the pupils to generalize the conclusion, and an attempted generalization, followed by criticism, suggestion and refinement led to a statement of the *general* theorem which was accepted by all the pupils. There had already been agreement that "the converse of a definition is acceptable authority" and following these theorems on parallel lines the teacher raised the question whether the converse of a theorem was also acceptable authority. Many pupils believed that the converse of theorems should be accepted, but the converse of such propositions as:

> If a man lives in Columbus then he lives in Ohio.
> All right angles are equal angles.
> If a man is rich then he can buy a car.

impressed all of them with the necessity of proving a converse before it can become an acceptable authority. The converse of each theorem already established was stated and most of them were proved.

These theorems were regarded by the pupils as *implications* of the definitions and assumptions they had made. Each pupil reserved a section of his text for "Implications of Definitions and Assumptions" and in this section placed all the implications which he established, giving the proof and generalized statement for each of these theorems. Wherever possible, corresponding three-dimensional concepts were considered and many properties of Euclidean space were thus accepted. The real purpose of this extension into space was to give the pupils an opportunity to visualize three-dimensional figures and, in general, no proofs were given. However, three of the pupils became greatly interested in this three-dimensional work and did prove a large number of theorems concerning the properties of space.

The teacher had a definite purpose in directing the thought of the pupils to the relation between the two angles on the same side of a transversal which intersected two parallel lines. With Figure I on the board—

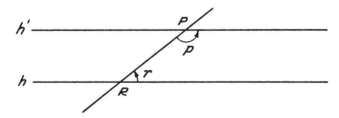

Fig. I

he asked the pupils to assume that h and h' were parallel and to write down all the resulting implications. Among these was the statement that angle p + angle r = 180°. He then asked them to assume that h is fixed in position but that h' rotates around the fixed point P. Much emphasis was placed on the fact that the slightest rotation of h' to either the right or the left brings into the finite plane and under control a point which, when the lines are parallel, is beyond control. It is the point at which h' will intersect h, and although it may be at a very great distance from R the assumption that non-parallel lines in the same plane intersect defines its existence. The pupils participated in this discussion and to a large extent guided this development by their questions and contributions. The teacher suggested that they study what happens when the rotating line h' takes a position such as that indicated by the dotted line h'' in Figure 2. The point

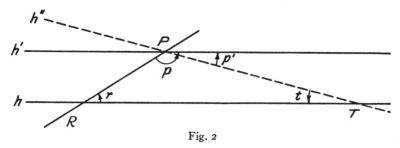

Fig. 2

T was thus defined and a pupil pointed out that PRT is a triangle. Another pupil said, "How do you know? Triangle has not yet been defined." The definition of triangle earlier accepted but never used was then recalled, and when a pupil pointed out that a diagram consisting of two parallel lines cut by a transversal might be considered "a figure with three lines as sides" the original definition was changed to read:

A triangle is a closed figure with three lines as sides.

The teacher then raised the question of what happened to angle p as the line h' rotated around P in the direction indicated. The pupils promptly agreed that the angle p was made smaller by the amount of rotation but that with the rotation there appeared in the figure a new angle t whose size was always equal to the amount by which angle p was decreased. Thus, if angle p is decreased by p' then $t = p'$ because h'' is a transversal cutting the parallel lines h and h' and the alternate interior angles of parallel lines are equal. Since angle r is constant and since the decrease of angle p is exactly balanced by the increase of angle t, there was unanimous approval of the statement that angle $r +$ angle $RPT +$ angle $t = 180°$.

After a further study of this figure, including the changes that occur as h' makes one complete revolution about P, the pupils were asked to draw any triangle and see what they could discover about the sum of the angles of that particular triangle. All of them felt that the sum was 180° but no one knew, at first, just how to proceed to demonstrate this fact. However, after thoughtful study followed by a suggestion from the teacher that reference to the diagram of the preceding discussion might prove helpful, there was increasing evidence from all parts of the room that discoveries were being made, and before the class period was over seventeen of the twenty-four pupils present had worked out an "acceptable" proof for the theorem concerning the sum of the angles of a triangle.

The only real weakness in each of these seventeen proofs was found in the statements relating to the drawing of the auxiliary line through one of the vertices. All the pupils felt the need for such a line and all of them drew it. However, twelve of them said nothing whatever as to where this line came from or how it was drawn, although in the remainder of the proof it was assumed to be parallel to the side opposite the vertex through which it was drawn. Four of the pupils did say that the line was drawn parallel to whatever the name of the side happened to be, but did not say that this line was to be drawn through any particular vertex; nor did they feel the need for any authority to support this construction. In the proof of only one pupil was the statement "Draw a line through A in such a way that it is parallel to BC" and as an authority he gave "any helping line can be drawn."

These proofs are called "acceptable" because in each of them the basic mathematical ideas are acceptable. Their weakness lies in lack of precise and accurate statement. All of them, however, served as excellent illustrations of the way in which unrecognized assumptions can creep into one's thinking and definitely affect conclusions. The pupils were impressed and, in the judgment of the writer, greatly helped by the discussion on this point and wanted to make explicit those assumptions which were implicit in their proofs. It was thus that the famous parallel postulate of Euclid was approached. The various statements of this assumption that were made before it was expressed in a form acceptable to all are interesting. The original statement, which is the first of those given below, was criticized, improved and further improved as indicated by those statements which follow it:

A line can be drawn parallel to another line.

Through any point a line can be drawn parallel to another line.

Through any point not on a given line it is possible to draw a line parallel to the given line.

Through a given point not on a given line it is possible to draw one and only one line parallel to the given line.

Enough of the history of Euclid's assumption was discussed to stimulate and retain the interest of the pupils and also to give them some background for the later discussion of the assumptions which led to non-Euclidean geometries. As a generalization of this theorem one pupil volunteered the statement:

The angles of a triangle equal 180°.

and a number of the pupils agreed with this statement. Other pupils, however, suggested that it be revised to read:

The sum of the angles of any triangle is 180°,

and as an illustration of the critical manner in which the pupils were thinking still another suggested that "in order to be more accurate" this general statement should be:

The sum of the interior angles of any triangle is 180°.

To this there was unanimous agreement and the complete proof of the theorem, followed by the general statement, was placed in each textbook in whatever form seemed logical to the individual pupil concerned and best suited his abilities.

At this point, it will be helpful to summarize the general principles and methods by which "implications of definitions and assumptions" or "theorems" are discovered. If the pupil is to have the opportunity "to reason about the subject matter of geometry in his own way," no theorem should be stated in advance; for such a statement fixes, to some extent, the direction of his thought and deprives him of discovering for himself the mathematical relations which control a situation. While in some cases assistance is certain to be needed the teacher should consider himself nothing more than a guide who directs *toward* the discovery and develops within the pupil increasing power to discover for himself. The general principles and methods which were followed in developing this sense of discovery and which are inherent in all preceding illustrations are summarized below:

1. No formal text is used. Each pupil writes his own text as the work develops and is able to express his own individuality in organization, in arrangement, in clarity of presentation and in the kind and number of implications established.

2. The statement of what is to be proved is not given the pupil. Certain properties of a figure are assumed and the pupil is given an opportunity to discover the implications of these assumed properties.

3. No generalized statement is made before the pupil has had an opportunity to think about the particular properties assumed. This generalization is made by the pupil after he has discovered it.

4. Through the assumptions made the attention of all pupils is directed toward the discovery of a few theorems which seem important to the teacher.

5. Assumptions leading to theorems that are relatively unimportant are suggested in mimeographed material which is available to all pupils but not required of any.

6. The major emphasis is not on the statement proved, but rather on the *method of proof*.

7. The extent to which pupils profit from the guidance of the teacher varies with the pupil and the supervised study periods are particularly helpful in making it possible to care for these variations. In addition individual conferences are planned when advisable.

Teachers who are "concerned not merely by the objective goals reached by the pupils, but quite as truly with the actual searchings themselves," will recognize that when the suggestions in 2 and 3 are translated into actual classroom practice the opportunity for discovery, to which so many teachers of mathematics lend verbal allegiance, is preserved for the pupil. Also, the suggestions in 4 and 5 make it possible for each pupil to develop "whatever sequence will give him the greatest sense of accomplishment," and while, as indicated in 4, there is a small number of theorems which constitute a common background for all pupils and which serve as illustrations of what proof really means, provision is made for original work commensurate with the abilities and interests of each individual pupil. Frequently, the original work of one pupil is of such a character that it has very real value for all others, and in such cases it is presented by the pupil to the group for criticism and discussion.

In order that the principles discussed in the preceding paragraph may be still further clarified, an actual illustration may be helpful. However, to appreciate the significance of this illustration it is essential that the experiences of the class preceding this illustration be explained. Parallel lines had been defined as "lines having the same amount and direction of rotation from a line which intersects them," and the following theorems were common to the experience of all pupils:

> If two parallel lines are cut by a transversal, the alternate interior angles are equal.
>
> If two parallel lines are cut by a transversal, the two interior angles on the same side of the transversal are supplementary.
>
> If two lines in the same plane are cut by a transversal and if the alternate interior angles are equal, then the two lines are parallel.
>
> The sum of the interior angles of a triangle is 180°.

A number of pupils had established many other properties of parallels but only the four theorems above had been proved by all pupils. Congruence had been discussed and defined and a consideration of the conditions which made triangles congruent had led to the acceptance of the following assumptions:

> If two triangles have two angles and the included side of one equal respectively to two angles and the included side of the other, then the triangles are congruent.

If two triangles have two sides and the included angle of one equal respectively to two sides and the included angle of the other, then the triangles are congruent.

With only this background in common the pupils were working during a period of supervised study on whatever seemed most important to them at that particular time. Some were bringing their textbooks up to date, some were analyzing certain types of non-mathematical material which claimed their interest, while some were investigating one set of assumptions and some another. Among the situations available was one which related to the accompanying figure. The suggestions given were as follows:

1. Assume that angle a = angle a'. What are the resulting implications?

2. Assume in addition that angle b = angle c, and study the figure for any added implications.

3. Now combine with the two preceding assumptions the additional assumption that $BH = KC$ and try to discover what additional properties are implied.

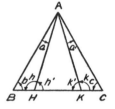

The teacher observed that a number of pupils were working on this exercise and he also observed that the variation in results offered an excellent opportunity for general discussion. He therefore asked that all students direct their attention to a consideration of these results, which were presented to the group by the individual pupils concerned. This proved to be a most profitable discussion and revealed in a rather impressive manner the cumulative effect of additional assumptions. Following the assumption in 2, some pupils reported that triangles ABH and AKC had the same shape, but no one made any attempt to show any line segments equal until the third assumption was available. One pupil, however, who had given no previous thought to this set of assumptions, raised the question whether it was necessary to prove any triangles congruent to show that $AH = AK$. He said he believed this followed at once from the assumption in 2 for that assumption did imply that angle h' = angle k' and "if those angles are equal, the sides opposite them would have to be equal." Other pupils supported this statement but all felt that it must be proved before it could be accepted. No one suggested that it be recognized as an assumption.

At the close of the period three pupils went to the teacher's office and worked independently in an effort to prove this conclusion. Two of them were successful, and the next session of the class opened with one of these pupils presenting his proof to the entire group. He met some resistance, particularly from those who themselves had been unable to discover a proof, and the nature of their criticism reveals the quality of their thought. When the bisector of angle HAK was drawn the question was raised whether an angle could be bisected and whether or not this bisector had to intersect HK. These criticisms resulted in healthy discussion, and as an outgrowth of this discussion the following assumptions, which were implicit in the proof but previously unrecognized, were accepted:

It is possible to draw a line bisecting an angle.

A line bisecting an angle of a triangle must intersect the opposite side.

Here, then, is an illustration of how a question raised by one pupil led to the proof of the general theorem that:

If two angles of a triangle are equal, the sides opposite those angles are equal,

even before the "isosceles triangle" had been defined. The converse of this theorem was suggested almost immediately and was proved without serious difficulty by most members of the class.

INDUCTIVE PROOF

The insertion of the word "interior" in the general statement of the theorem dealing with the sum of the angles of a triangle led many pupils to ask if a triangle had "any exterior angles." Illustrations of exterior angles were thereupon given to them and a definition of this concept was derived from a study of these illustrations. The question was immediately raised: "What is the sum of the exterior angles?" and this led to a consideration of what was meant by extending the sides "in succession." The pupils then discovered the sum of the exterior angles to be 360° and most of them made the following generalization:

> The sum of the exterior angles of a triangle is twice the sum of the interior angles.

The idea of studying the sum of the angles of a figure of more than three sides apparently occurred to none of the pupils, but since the teacher desired to use this opportunity to emphasize the nature of induction, he raised the question as to how the sum of the interior angles of a four-sided figure might be found. No further suggestion was needed. The pupils recognized the possibilities, and figures with various numbers of sides were drawn on the board. The teacher suggested that in studying the sum of the angles of these different figures it would be helpful to arrange the work in tabular form, and outlined a table for this purpose. While some pupils generalized after only two cases, there were some who failed to recognize the nature of the process and did not generalize at all. Individual conferences with these pupils seemed advisable for the purpose of clarifying this method of reaching generalizations.

As an outgrowth of this work "diagonal" and "polygon" were defined as well as some of the more commonly used special polygons, such as "quadrilateral, pentagon, hexagon" and the like. No pupil had apparently given any thought to the sum of the exterior angles of these polygons, and in reply to a question concerning the sum of the exterior angles of a quadrilateral practically all of the pupils indicated that this sum would be *more* than the sum of the exterior angles of a triangle.

Further questions revealed that this conclusion was related in their thinking to the idea that "the greater the number of sides, the greater the sum of the angles." As they gave more thought to this problem, however, some became more cautious while others became more certain. This latter group argued that:

> Since the sum of the exterior angles of a triangle is twice the sum of the interior angles, then the sum of the exterior angles of a quadrilateral must be 720°.

Discussion led to an explicit statement of the assumption on which this generalization was based, and the teacher used this as a further illustration of how hidden assumptions affect conclusions. Some of the more careful thinkers had by this time found the required sum and all were surprised that it was the same as that for the exterior angles of a triangle. Following a similar investigation by each pupil of the exterior angles of a pentagon, most of them were ready to accept the generalization:

> If the sides of any polygon are extended in succession, the sum of the exterior angles thus formed is 360°.

The pupils realized that here was a "new way of reaching generalizations" and the nature of this new process was examined in detail. Many illustrations of induction were given by different pupils, and the teacher added others which were drawn from various fields of thought but particularly from the sciences. Among these illustrations were some which showed the failure of induction, and the dangers and limitations of this new method of thought were recognized. As an outgrowth of this discussion the following general principles were accepted:

> *Induction* is the process of reaching a general conclusion through the study of particular cases.
>
> No one can be certain that conclusions established by induction are true. They are only probably true and the probability increases with an increase in the number of cases for which the conclusion is shown to be true.
>
> The validity of the generalization is destroyed if only one instance can be shown where it does not hold.
>
> A conclusion established by induction depends on the assumption that all cases which have not been studied are just like those which have been studied.

While the pupils were fairly cautious in accepting the absolute certainty of conclusions established by deduction, all of them felt that they were "much more certain" than those established by induction. This is, it seems to the writer, a most significant point, for in the course of the same discussion in which the above principles were abstracted from the general process there was agreement with the pupil who said, "Our assumptions are established by induction," which means that these assumptions have only probability in their favor.

It seems, then, that at this time the pupils failed to realize the logical relation between conclusions reached deductively and the assumptions which imply these conclusions, for how can conclusions reached deductively be any "more certain" than the assumptions on which they depend? Argument by induction is not limited to the field of mathematics, and if this method of thought is to be learned "in connection with the field to which transfer is desired," the pupil should be provided with an opportunity to analyze such arguments in non-mathematical situations. It often occurs that an editorial writer uses induction in an effort to establish his major thesis. The following exercise illustrates one way in which editorials using this "method of proof" can be used to advantage:

Following the world war the government of the United States gave to every eligible soldier who applied for it an adjusted compensation certificate which is commonly known as "the bonus." The certificate provided that this bonus would be paid in 1945, but ever since it was made available to the veterans the Congress has been subjected to almost constant pressure that this bonus be paid without further delay. On numerous occasions bills have been passed by both houses of Congress, conforming to the veterans' request for immediate cash payment, only to be vetoed by the President. However, both the House of Representatives and the Senate recently passed such a bill over the President's veto and on January 27, 1936, immediate cash payment of the bonus became the law of the land. It is believed by many people that a large number of representatives and senators voted to pay this bonus even though such a vote was against their own personal belief as to what was best for the country as a whole. They felt that their own political future depended on retaining the good will of the soldiers and they did not wish to antagonize this highly organized group. In a recent editorial, however, a distinguished writer states the following proposition:

"Senators who voted against immediate payment of the bonus are not usually defeated when running for reelection."

and in an effort to establish the truth of this proposition in the minds of the readers says:

" 1. The interesting experience of two senators who have twice voted against the bonus, once with an election right ahead of them, seems to prove the proposition and also that members in Congress with nerve enough to stand up do not really suffer at the polls.

2. One of these senators is a Democrat, Edward Raymond Burke of Nebraska. The facts about Senator Burke are these: In 1934

he was a member of the House and the only man in the Nebraska delegation to vote against the bonus.

3. It was his first term and he was warned by his colleagues what would happen to him. After the session was over Mr. Burke went back to Omaha and one day met a professional leader of the veterans on the street.

4. 'All right, Burke,' he was told, 'you went back on us, didn't you? Well, you're through. You can't go back to the House.'

5. 'Isn't that interesting?' said Senator Burke. 'In that case I shall run for the Senate,' which he did, was elected, voted against the bonus again two weeks ago, and also voted to sustain the veto of the President. The most interesting part of this incident, however, is that not one of Senator Burke's four Nebraska pro-bonus colleagues of 1934 is now in public life. One was beaten in the primaries, one in the general election, one retired and the other made an unsuccessful fight for governor.

6. The story of Republican Senator Arthur H. Vandenberg of Michigan is equally interesting. In 1934, just ahead of his campaign for reelection, Senator Vandenberg voted against the bonus and also to sustain the 1934 veto. He was never asked a question until his final meeting, held in Detroit.

7. Then a veteran arose and asked him why. Senator Vandenberg gave his reasons and the veteran replied, 'Well, Senator, I don't agree with you but I must say you gave me an honest answer.' Senator Vandenberg thinks he gained votes rather than lost them on this issue.

8. At any rate, he was reelected and is now recognized as a Republican aspirant for the presidency. In spite of this he recently voted against the bonus and also upheld the presidential veto.

9. The 'scare cat' senators who vote entirely through fear and against their own convictions might well ponder on the political experiences of Senators Burke and Vandenberg in voting against rather than with the organized minorities."

The writer of this editorial apparently believes that he has established the truth of his proposition. Do you agree with him? Assuming that the facts he has presented are reliable, is his conclusion justified? By what process of reasoning did he arrive at his conclusion? If you do not feel that his argument is convincing, can you point out the weakness in it? Do you think this argument would lead a senator to vote according to his convictions in a similar situation? Discuss the argument and in your discussion consider these points which have been raised. The paragraphs are numbered for your convenience if you wish to refer to them.

The pupils were quick to point out the limitations of the argument used in this editorial, although they felt that it might be quite convincing to any reader who did not understand the nature of an inductive proof. One thing which emphasized the weakness of this argument more than anything else was the suggestion of one pupil that if "Senator Burke" and "Senator Vandenberg" were replaced by the names of two senators who had voted against immediate payment of the bonus and who had been defeated when running for re-election, the argument would be just as potent in proving the opposite proposition.

A number of editorials concerning the controversy over the suggested enlargement of the Supreme Court of the United States are excellent illustrations of an attempt to prove a broad generalization by induction. One writer, for example, states as his main proposition that:

Men do not deteriorate at the age of 70.

and evidence which he presents in support of this proposition consists of the following statements:

Senator Norris is a power in the senate at the age of 76.

Senator Glass has great national influence at the age of 75.

The Vice President of the United States is 75.

Elihu Root became a world figure after he was 70.

Stanley Baldwin, that steady rock of England during these perilous days when clear vision is demanded, will be 70 in August.

Pope Pius, whose view of facts certainly is not blurred, carries on successfully at the age of 80.

Benjamin Franklin's greatest work was done after he was 70.

Gladstone was called to the prime ministership of England three times after he was 70.

Von Hindenburg was drafted to save Germany in her darkest days when he was elected president after he had passed 80.

An argument of this type offers many possibilities to a teacher who is interested in leading his pupils to understand the nature of proof, and can be used to particular advantage with relation to induction. Does this writer really prove the proposition he apparently wants to establish? Are the statements in his argument likely to be accepted as facts by all people? Is there any weakness in the argument? If so, what is it? A consideration of questions of this sort will emphasize important points in connection with any argument, the pupils will be interested and their "reflective thinking" improved.

Another writer of some note presented an argument in support of the proposition that:

Once an amendment to the constitution has been submitted to the people, the time required for ratification is slightly over a year.

When stripped of verbiage, much of which was irrelevant to the proposition, his argument consisted of the following facts:

The eighteenth amendment was ratified in 13 months.
The nineteenth amendment was ratified in 15 months.
The twentieth amendment was ratified in 11 months.
The twenty-first amendment was ratified in 9½ months.

After generalizing from these four cases the writer mentions the child labor amendment, which up to the present time has failed of ratification, and refers to it as "the exception which proves the rule" whereas actually it is the exception which destroys the generalization. Arguments of this sort, which can be found on almost any editorial page, offer an excellent opportunity to show young people how the kind of thinking which is applied to idealized concepts in mathematics can become distorted when applied to concepts which tend to stir one's prejudices.

DETECTING THE FACTORS WHICH DETERMINE CONCLUSIONS

While the ability to gather pertinent evidence in support of a proposition, and to present it clearly, logically and effectively is one mark of an educated person, it is equally important to be able to analyze evidence presented by others in support of conclusions one is pressed to accept. To understand the nature of proof as defined on page 10 of this study is to know that these conclusions are "true" only within the limits of the assumptions on which they depend and to be able to detect these assumptions is an important attribute of "reflective thinking." At the beginning of each college year, for example, Professor Harold Hotelling[2] of Columbia University presents to his class in mathematical economics a mathematical demonstration of the proposition that "if everyone is left to himself and will just pursue vigorously his

[2] Harold Hotelling, "Some Little Known Applications of Mathematics," *The Mathematics Teacher*, Vol. xxix, No. 4, 1936, pp. 157–169.

own maximum profit, then everybody will be as well off as possible." His purpose in doing that, he says, "is not to make people believe in the proposition but to show what definitions and what assumptions have to be made in order to make a mathematical proof possible. By the time a person has understood the definitions and assumptions involved in these proofs, he is quite willing to reject the result."

As an illustration of the way in which the analysis of evidence serves to make explicit the basic factors on which a conclusion depends, the teacher guided the pupils in an examination of a proof for the theorem that "if two parallel lines are cut by a transversal, the two interior angles on the same side of the transversal are supplementary." The assumptions and definitions which determine this conclusion were explicitly stated and the undefined terms involved were recognized as essential to the proof. With this illustration as a guide the pupils were asked to analyze the evidence supporting the theorem that "The sum of the interior angles of a triangle is 180°," which the teacher selected for a definite purpose. While the factors which determine what the sum of these angles will be were presented in various ways, the following arrangement suggested by a pupil perhaps indicates better than any other the nature of the relation between the conclusion and the factors which imply it:

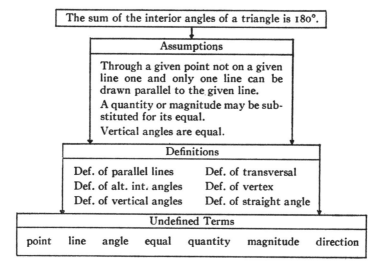

This analysis clearly revealed that one proof of this theorem, so important in the field of mathematics, actually depends on three assumptions, six definitions and seven undefined terms. The question was then raised as to who made these assumptions, who made the definitions and who selected the undefined terms? From these considerations the pupils realized that the sum of the interior angles of a triangle was not fixed by some divine power, for it was they who made these definitions and assumptions and it was they who selected the undefined terms. They disagreed with the statement of Edward Everett who wrote in 1870 that "In the pure mathematics we contemplate absolute truths, which existed in the divine mind before the morning stars sang together, and which will continue to exist there, when the last of their radiant host shall have fallen from heaven."[3] They saw that it was their own minds and not "the divine mind" that had manufactured this so-called "truth" about the sum of the angles of a triangle, and they recognized that this "truth" was relative to the factors which imply it.

The way in which the pupils had been introduced to the nature of assumptions was helpful in leading them to see that a change in any one of the three assumptions on which this conclusion depends would be likely to change the conclusion. In order to relate this to the space in which we live the teacher raised such questions as the following for the pupils' consideration:

"Is each of these assumptions validated by your own experience of actual space?"

"Which of these assumptions do you consider to be the most complex?"

"Do any of them have definite implications concerning the nature of space?"

There was no question in the mind of any pupil concerning the validity of these assumptions. The pupils felt that they squared with their own experience and "they must be valid because they work." There was general agreement that the first was the most complex "because it contains the greatest number of ideas," and there was uncertainty and doubt as to the implications of any of these assumptions "concerning

[3] Eric T. Bell, *The Queen of the Sciences*, p. 20. The Williams and Wilkins Co., Baltimore, 1931.

the nature of space." The teacher then recalled the assumption that "A line could be extended in either direction just as far as you want to extend it," and raised the question whether this assumption would be valid in a finite space. Furthermore, if space is finite and parallel lines are lines in the same plane that do not meet in the space in which they are drawn, might it not be possible to draw through a point more than one line parallel to a given line?

The history of the parallel postulate was now considered in greater detail and the teacher acquainted the pupils with the nature of the work done by Saccheri, Lobatchewsky, Bolyai and Riemann.[4] They learned what it meant to "challenge an assumption," and other important results which had been derived from questioning what had seemed "obvious" were discussed, such as the far-reaching consequences of Einstein's challenge of the axiom of the simultaneity of events.

Through such considerations, it became increasingly apparent to the pupils that the assumptions which they had selected and which had seemed "obvious to them" were not inherent in the nature of space. They realized that in their choice of assumptions they were really defining space, and this was a most surprising idea to them. They became conscious of the important fact that there was no way of telling whether their world actually corresponds to the assumptions they had selected or to those of Lobatchewsky or Riemann. To know which set of assumptions is "true" is relatively unimportant, even if that were possible, but it is very important for the pupil to recognize that these assumptions, whether they be those of Euclid, Lobatchewsky or Riemann, are in fact nothing more than agreements about an abstract space and that it is not possible to establish by logical proof any properties of that space which are not contdaine in the assumptions.

In the judgment of the writer, this analysis of the proof for the theorem concerning the sum of the interior angles of

[4] References helpful to the pupils are:
Vera Sanford, *A Short History of Mathematics*. Houghton Mifflin Co., 1930.
David Eugene Smith, *History of Mathematics*, Vol. 2. Ginn and Co., 1925.
Lillian Lieber, *Three Moons in Mathesis*. Brooklyn, 258 Clinton Ave.
Edwin E. Slosson, *Easy Lessons in Einstein*. Harcourt, Brace and Co., 1920.
Eric T. Bell, *Men of Mathematics*. Simon and Schuster, 1937.

a triangle, followed by a consideration of the important developments connected with the parallel postulate, was most helpful in broadening the understanding of each pupil as to the real nature of deductive proof. It revealed in an impressive manner how a change in only one assumption can change a conclusion, and the "truth" of a conclusion was now a question of *consistency* rather than one of absolute verity. It extended the thinking of the pupils beyond the limits of the Euclidean world and introduced them to the non-Euclidean worlds of Lobatchewsky, Riemann and Einstein. It stimulated their imagination and liberated their thinking just as the work of Lobatchewsky revolutionized the thinking of the early nineteenth century.

THE RECOGNITION OF ASSUMPTIONS IN NON-MATHEMATICAL ARGUMENTS

While a very large majority of the people in the United States will never be faced with the necessity of analyzing the evidence presented in support of a mathematical theorem, no thoughtful citizen of a democracy can avoid the necessity of examining the evidence in support of the great variety of conclusions he is pressed to accept. There has probably never been a time in the long history of human thought when the ability to detect the hidden assumptions in an argument and to recognize the "weasel words and phrases" was more to be desired than at present. No evidence is available to show that this generalized ability will be developed through the study of mathematics alone. It must be developed "in connection with the fields to which transfer is desired." To provide for this need many exercises similar to those which follow were given the pupils:

The fact that Thomas Jefferson was one of America's great mathematicians is known to comparatively few people although one might recognize his mathematical talent from a study of the Declaration of Independence of which he is the author. While this document, as we know it, was accepted and approved by fifty-six men, they did not change the general form which closely resembles that of a mathematical treatise. Will you analyze this document, using the following questions as guides in your consideration of it:

1. What are the assumptions to which the fifty-six men who signed this document agreed?

2. What generalization is made about George III, who at that time was the British king, and what sort of argument is used in an attempt to "prove" this generalization?
3. What conclusions are reached? Are these conclusions consistent with the assumptions?
4. Are these conclusions reached by induction or by deduction?

The kind of thinking which the pupils had been doing from the very beginning of this work was definitely reflected in these analyses and it was still more apparent in the discussion which followed. Such points as the following were raised by the pupils:

"Would the history of the United States have been changed if the assumption had been that 'All white men are created equal'?"

"How is 'equal' defined?"

"I do not accept the assumption that 'All men are created equal'."

"Was 'men' defined so as to include the Negro?"

"In the phrase 'certain inalienable rights' the word 'certain' should be defined to explain what these rights are."

"To assume that governments 'derive their just powers from the consent of the governed' implies democracy."

"Who is going to define what 'just powers' are?"

These illustrations, some of them taken from the papers of pupils and some from oral discussion in class, do not exhaust all the points made but they do offer some indication of the extent to which the thinking of the pupils had been affected by their growing understanding of the nature of proof.

The kind of advertising to which students are daily exposed is another fertile field in which to find situations which involve the idea of proof. Behind every advertisement is a multitude of assumptions. Once these assumptions are stated explicitly the advertisement loses a large part of its appeal. An illustration of this type follows:

While reading a magazine Helen's attention was drawn to the picture of a beautiful girl with an attractive smile who was represented as saying:

"I'd wished a thousand times for a brighter smile. One tube of Colgate's gave it to me. It was so annoying to see other girls with lovely smiles get all the dates. Then I tried Colgate's. Now my smiles are bright too."

This is really an argument for using Colgate's Dental Cream. The argument is based on certain assumptions. What are these assumptions? List them in the space below:

(Space was left here for the statement of the assumptions.)

Rate this argument as excellent, good, fair, poor, very poor, using whichever word in your opinion best describes it:

_____Rating

Numerous exercises of this kind, varied somewhat to suit the type of advertisement considered, have impressed the pupil with the need for evidence "in support of any conclusion he is pressed to accept"; have helped him to "analyze that evidence," "to recognize both the stated and the unstated assumptions" essential to the conclusions, and "to evaluate the argument." There follows another illustration of the type which involves the added feature of "evaluating the assumptions, accepting some and rejecting others":

While reading a magazine one evening, John's attention was drawn to the picture of a fountain pen. Underneath the picture he read these words:

"A brain harassed by a pen that runs dry loses its brilliance, power and expression. Hence we have created a pen with 102 per cent more ink capacity and visible ink supply."

These statements seemed to impress him. He had always been irritated when his pen went dry but he had never before realized the extent to which this affected "the brilliance, power and expression" of his brain. He determined he would own this new pen "with 102 per cent more ink capacity" and on the next day he purchased it. What assumptions are involved in the argument which led him to this conclusion? Write them below, placing a plus sign before those which you accept and a minus sign before those which you reject:

(Space was left here for the statement of the assumptions.)

Using these assumptions as authorities, prepare in logical form the argument suggested in the above advertisement for the purchase of this pen:

(Space was left here for the presentation of the argument.)

Would this argument alone influence you to buy the pen?

Answer: _____

Evidence that this kind of exercise had a helpful influence on the ability of the pupils to detect assumptions and to make them more resistant to the power of advertising and other types of propaganda is given in Chapter V.

It very often occurs that different people who use the same laws of thought and who reason clearly and logically about a given problem reach different conclusions. The point is raised in the following illustration which in other respects is similar to those that precede it:

By a decision of 6 to 3 the Supreme Court of the United States recently declared the Agricultural Adjustment Act of the New Deal to be unconstitutional. This created wide discussion among people in various walks of life. The viewpoints of a distinguished group of gentlemen who discussed this decision have been summarized by a local paper in the following proposition:

"It is regrettable that the United States Constitution in its present form is inadequate to meet the needs of present day agriculture and government procedure."

Let us consider that this summary is dependable and that it expresses their real belief. They have reached this belief by making a number of assumptions. What are some of them? Give as many as you can in the space below:

(Space was left here for the list of assumptions.)

It is possible that if these gentlemen could examine the assumptions on which their belief depends they might reject some of them and thus change their conclusions. Do you accept all the assumptions which you have listed? If not, which do you reject? Indicate those you reject by placing a minus sign before them.

It is worth while to note that three of the justices considered the A.A.A. constitutional while six of them did not. As one writer says, they reached their decision "without emotion, without prejudice and through the clear light of logic." One might expect "the clear light of logic" to yield a decision which would be unanimous. How do you account for the fact that three of these distinguished gentlemen found the act constitutional while six of them ruled otherwise? Discuss this on the other side of the paper.

In addition to the other values already considered, this type of exercise serves to emphasize the point that different assumptions are likely to lead to different conclusions when these conclusions are reached "without emotion, without prejudice and through the clear light of logic."

Many people who exhibit great mental power when dealing with mathematical concepts fail to think clearly when controversial issues are under consideration. A local problem involving such an issue and one which claimed the eager interest of all pupils is summarized in the following exercise:

A group of citizens in a certain Columbus precinct met all the legal requirements to have a local option vote on Tuesday, November 5, 1935, the day of the general State election. The purpose of this vote was to find out whether or not the majority of the citizens in that precinct favored the continued sale of intoxicating liquor in the district. The "wets" charged that "the election should be prevented" and appealed to the County Judge for an injunction which would stop it. The argument they presented ran somewhat as follows:

Argument	Statement of Fact	Assumption
It was necessary to file a petition to hold this election. The last day this petition could be legally filed was October 4.		
A citizen must register if he is to qualify as a voter.		
The "drys" did not file their petition until October 4.		
By October 4 all the "drys" had registered.		
After filing of the petition only a day and a half remained in which the "wets" could register.		
Because of this lack of time all the "wets" were unable to register.		
Nothing should interfere with a citizen's right to register.		
Therefore the injuncton should be granted and the election stopped.		

It is probable that no other issue is more conducive to prejudice than the liquor issue and when prejudice replaces reason, conclusions are not likely to be reliable. Lay aside any prejudice you may have on this particular issue and consider the argument by the "wets" only on its merits. By checking in the proper column indicate which of the statements in the argument you believe to be facts and those which you believe to be assumptions. Do you find that the argument is sound? In your opinion are the assumptions justified? It is not necessary to be a county judge to determine the validity of this argument. Suppose you were in the position of the judge. Considering the argument alone, what would be your answer to this request for an injunction to stop the election? In the space below present your decision as the conclusion of a logically developed argument, the conclusion being either "Therefore the injunction is granted" or "Therefore the injunction is not granted."

In evaluating the argument presented by the "wets" the pupil not only must distinguish "facts" from "assumptions" but he must be able to detect the important assumptions which are essential to an honest conclusion and which are not explicitly stated in the argument. He then places himself in the position of the county judge, evaluates these assumptions, either denies or grants the injunction and presents a "logically developed argument" supporting his position. This proved to be one of the most profitable exercises considered.

The purpose of an editorial writer, in general, is to convert the reader to a definite point of view. To do this he usually states a major proposition and then presents evidence which, in his opinion, should lead the reader to accept the proposition. Editorials of this kind are excellent material for t he consideration of any class interested in the study of "proof. " An exercise built around such an editorial follows:

During the latter part of October, 1935, the corn-hog farmers of the United States were asked for an expression of opinion as to whether or not they desired the continuation of the Agricultural Adjustment Act. The result of this referendum seemed to indicate that they did favor this program by a majority of about 8 to 1. In considering this, however, a distinguished writer recently stated the following proposition:

"It is surprising that any votes were cast against the continuation of the policies of the A.A.A."

and in attempting to establish this proposition he presents the following discussion:

" 1. Today there is country-wide wonder that any votes were cast in opposition to the referendum which brought an 8 to 1 victory to the A.A.A.

2. For the Roosevelt administration did not present both sides of the argument to the corn-hog farmers, but merely asked whether they would continue to favor crop control and a subsidy.

3. The consumers who have to pay, in the cost of living, higher prices for foodstuffs, were not asked to vote.

4. None of the arguments that might be made on the faulty economics of the A.A.A.'s policies was presented to the corn-hog farmer. It was a one-sided election among a group who were really being asked whether they would like to have a better price for their

product by limiting the output of their farms and making their products relatively scarce.

5. When steel manufacturers used to get together and try to agree among themselves on limitation of production and prices, the government used to call it a trust and apply the anti-trust laws. But farm organizations of all kinds are exempt from the operation of anti-trust laws and the A.A.A. is really a substitute for the old-fashioned trust or monopoly, but with governmental control.

6. The spectacle of a government-managed election among the members of a minority group, whose decision now is to effect the prices paid by the majority, is still too novel for widespread appreciation of its implications. Minority by minority, the New Deal offers money benefits in the form of processing taxes or subsidies and the result is to build up a cumulative weapon of blocs for the presidential elections. Minorities swing national elections because they move from one party to the other, while the straight ticket voters remain indifferent.

7. If each powerful minority group is to be appealed to on grounds of direct benefit to it with funds either taken out of general taxation or by levying assessments on the cost of living, the chaotic consequences will hardly be called 'planned economy.' It will be difficult for any opposition political party to win in the near future on the simple truths that century-old experience has proved. It only means that New Deal economy may have to run its full course, bringing in its wake the friction that has always arisen between classes and the concussion that has always come from government control of production and price-fixing, no matter where it has been tried in human history.''

All of this discussion is not pertinent to the argument, for in it there is a good deal of the writer's own philosophy concerning government policies. What are the principal statements which in your opinion he uses to "prove" his proposition? Arrange these statements in what you believe to be a logical order and reconstruct his argument in the space below. Do not attempt to support these statements by any authorities but by placing a check mark in the proper column indicate which of them you believe to be statements of fact and those which you believe to be mere assumptions.

Argument	Statement of Fact	Assumption

(Sufficient space was left here for the presentation of the argument.)

In view of the argument which you have presented do you consider the conclusion justified? If you do not consider the conclusion justified by the argument, discuss your reason for this in the space that follows:

(Sufficient space was left here for the presentation of reasons.)

There are paragraphs in this discussion which appear to have no direct relation to the proposition which the writer really wanted to establish. Some of them are irrelevant to the argument, some are generalizations about the result of the referendum and some are inserted for other purposes. In the space below will you discuss briefly the nature of each of these paragraphs? They are numbered for convenient reference . . .

(Sufficient space was left here for the discussion.)

An exercise of this sort, while combining most of the features included in the preceding illustrations, has additional values. To analyze any discussion for the purpose of determining which statements support the major proposition and which are irrelevant is critical thinking of the most helpful sort. The reconstruction of the writer's argument, omitting all irrelevant statements, also proved to be a most revealing and profitable activity.

The exercise which follows is built around an event which had been discussed in the local papers and which had been given wide publicity:

Mrs. Lewis Seymour was recently struck by an automobile and instantly killed. The driver of the car did not stop and while a man saw the accident he failed to see the number of the license plates on the car. However, he did notice that the right headlight was broken and that a tire blew out at the time of the accident. He reported these facts to the police and twelve hours later they found a car with a flat tire and with the right headlight broken. This car was parked behind the house of Hezekiah Berry and belonged to him. Numerous conclusions considered by the police are stated below. Place a plus sign in column one opposite each conclusion which you will accept from a consideration of only the facts given above:

	I	2	3	4
a. It is certain that the car which struck Mrs. Seymour belonged to Hezekiah Berry....a.				
b. The given facts are irrelevant to the problem of discovering who owned the car that struck Mrs. Seymour.................b.				
c. It is certain that Hezekiah Berry was not driving the car that struck Mrs. Seymour..c.				
d. Other facts are needed before it can be definitely proved that Hezekiah Berry was the driver of the car that struck Mrs. Seymour...........................d.				
e. It is probable that the car that struck Mrs. Seymour belonged to Hezekiah Berry....e.				
f. It is certain that the car which struck Mrs. Seymour did not belong to Hezekiah Berry................................f.				
g. It is certain that Hezekiah Berry was the driver of the car that struck Mrs. Seymour................................g.				

Through further study of the problem the police found that the glass at the scene of the accident was of the same pattern as that in the broken headlight on Mr. Berry's car. Using this added fact in connection with those already given indicate in column two which of the preceding conclusions you would accept.

It was also established that when Mrs. Seymour was struck she was carrying a quart of potato soup. Some of this soup was found at the scene of the accident while traces of the same kind of soup were found on Mr. Berry's car. Does this added fact change your judgment as to which of the preceding conclusions you would accept? Indicate in column three those conclusions which you believe are now definitely established by the known facts.

The police also found strands of hair on the broken headlight of Mr. Berry's automobile. Now considering *all* of these facts will you indicate in column four which of the conclusions you believe to be justified.

Exercises of this type reveal the effect of cumulative evidence on the thinking of the pupil and indicate just how much and what sort of evidence is needed to change his acceptance of a conclusion from probability to certainty. Such work, when followed by thoughtful discussion, has a definite tendency to increase the caution of the pupils in reaching conclusions.

As an outgrowth of this kind of thinking some of the pupils became conscious of the fact that underlying their beliefs were many assumptions, and out of this came a request that the examination of these assumptions become a matter for group consideration. Many topics for such study were listed and from these an exercise similar to the following was prepared:

Underlying the beliefs of an individual are numerous assumptions, and anyone who accepts a conclusion regarding any issue at the same time accepts the assumptions on which that conclusion depends, even though he may not know what some of them really are. For this reason it is well that we often examine the assumptions behind our beliefs so that we may be fully conscious of just what our position on any important issue involves. Will you then state your present position on the following topics and in the space provided for analysis, list the statements on which in your opinion this position depends? By checking in the proper column indicate which of these statements you consider to be facts and those which you regard as assumptions. It will also be well for you to define any words or phrases which will help to clarify your position:

1. Racial Superiority.

Many people believe that the white races are superior to the colored races.

My present belief concerning this is:

Analysis of my belief	Statement of Fact	Assumption

2. Compulsory Education.

We have in this country certain laws which compel all young people up to a certain age to attend an organized school. Some people believe that such laws are most desirable, while others feel that their operation accomplishes little if anything in improving the quality of our citizenship.

My present belief concerning this is:

Analysis of my belief	Statement of Fact	Assumption

3. A Citizen's Obligation to His Government in Time of War.
Many people in the United States have recently stated that they would never bear arms in any war. Others feel that it is their duty to support their government at all times whether in peace or in war.
My position on this important issue is:

Analysis of my position	Statement of Fact	Assumption

4. Awards.
Some pupils in the school feel that there should be a set of fixed criteria for honors and awards, and once a student has satisfied these criteria, he should be granted an award. Others feel that the problem of awards is more complex, and that any set of fixed criteria cannot possibly take into account all factors in a given situation.
My present position on this problem is:

Analysis of my position	Statement of Fact	Assumption

Discussion of such questions as these was noticeably un-prejudiced. All of the results had been mimeographed and each pupil had before him the work of the others. Contrasting positions were considered and the assumptions underlying each of these positions were examined. The objective way in which the pupils went about this was particularly impressive. Many of them stated that such discussions were especially helpful in clarifying their own thinking and it is believed that all of them learned many valuable lessons of tolerance in their thoughtful consideration of these complex problems.

CHAPTER IV

GEOMETRIC CONTENT

NUMEROUS illustrations were given in the preceding chapter of the way in which undefined terms were selected, definitions made, and the need for assumptions recognized. This method of procedure resulted in general agreement concerning a group of these basic concepts which were common to the experience of all pupils and a continuation of these procedures yielded the following outcomes:

Terms Accepted by the Pupils as Undefined

angle	greater than	point
area	horizontal	quantity
between	inside	rotation
dihedral angle	less than	solid
direction	line	straight line
distance	magnitude	vertical
equal	outside	volume
fixed	plane	

Terms and Concepts Defined by the Pupils

acute angle	collinear points	distance from a point
adjacent angles	complementary angles	to a line
alternate angles	cone	distance from a point
altitude	congruent figures	to a plane
angle between line	coplanar points	equiangular
and plane	corresponding angles	equidistant
arc	cube	equilateral triangle
axis	curved line	exterior angle
base	cylinder	heptagon
base of isosceles	decagon	hexagon
triangle	degree	hypotenuse
bisect	diagonal	initial side
center of a circle	diameter	inscribed
central angle	distance between	inscribed angle
chord	parallel lines	interior angle
circle	distance between	intersecting lines
circumference	parallel planes	isosceles triangle
circumscribed		length of line segment

line parallel to a plane
line segment
line segments divided
  proportionally
locus
major arc
mean proportional
measure of a dihedral
  angle
minor arc
nonagon
obtuse angle
octagon
parallel lines
parallelogram
parallel planes
pentagon

perimeter
perpendicular lines
perpendicular planes
polygon
polyhedral angle
prism
proportion
pyramid
quadrilateral
radius
ratio
rectangle
rectangular solid
reflex angle
regular polygon
rhombus
right angle

right triangle
secant
semicircle
skew lines
similar figures
solids of revolution
square
straight angle
supplementary angles
tangent
terminal side
transversal
trapezoid
triangle
trihedral angle
vertex of an angle
vertical angles

In the general discussion and group thinking of the pupils all of these concepts were used in one form or another, and it was not until their meaning was clear that they were defined. These definitions were an outgrowth of the pupils' thinking and were not the basis for it. They were derived in precisely the same manner as were those in the illustrations of Chapter III. The original statements were often vague and misleading. These were corrected, improved, and refined until the meaning was precise even though awkwardly expressed.

Assumptions Made by the Pupils

There are points in space.

One and only one line can be drawn through any two points.

The shortest distance between two points is the straight line joining them.

A line can be extended in either direction just as far as one wants to extend it.

A line segment can be bisected at one and only one point.

If two straight lines intersect, they can intersect in one and only one point.

One and only one plane can be passed through three points which are not collinear.

An infinite number of planes can be passed through three points which are collinear.

One and only one plane can be passed through two intersecting lines.

One and only one plane can be passed through two parallel lines.

One and only one plane can be passed through a line and a point not on the line.

If a straight line is drawn in a plane, then all points on the line are in the plane.

If two planes intersect they can intersect in one and only one line.

Vertical angles are equal.

Vertical dihedral angles are equal.

If two lines intersect in such a manner that the adjacent angles are equal, then the two lines are perpendicular.

If two planes intersect in such a manner that the adjacent dihedral angles are equal, then the planes are perpendicular.

Through a given point not on a given line there is one and only one perpendicular to the given line.

Through any given point there is one and only one line perpendicular to a given plane.

Through a given point not on a given line it is possible to draw one and only one line parallel to the given line.

Through a given point not on a given plane it is possible to pass one and only one plane parallel to the given plane.

An infinite number of perpendiculars can be drawn to a given line at any given point on the line and these perpendiculars all lie in the plane perpendicular to the given line through the given point.

A quantity or magnitude may be substituted for its equal.

When equal quantities are added to equal quantities the sums are equal.

When equal quantities are subtracted from equal quantities the results are equal.

When equal quantities are multiplied by equal quantities the products are equal.

When equal quantities are divided by equals the quotients are equal except when the divisor is zero.

All straight angles are equal.

All right angles are equal.

The complements of equal angles are equal.

The supplements of equal angles are equal.

Any quantity or magnitude is equal to itself.

A definition when turned around is acceptable authority.

It is possible to draw one and only one line bisecting an angle.

A line bisecting an angle of a triangle must intersect the opposite side.

If two angles and the included side of one triangle are equal respectively to two angles and the included side of another triangle, then the triangles are congruent.

If two sides and the included angle of one triangle are equal respectively to two sides and the included angle of another triangle, then the triangles are congruent.

If the three sides of one triangle are equal respectively to the three sides of a second triangle, then the triangles are congruent.

Corresponding elements of congruent figures are equal.

A line can intersect a plane in one point only. If it has more than one point in common with the plane it must lie wholly in the plane.

If a line intersects one of two parallel lines, then it must intersect the other also.

One and only one circle can be drawn with any given center and any given radius.

All radii of a circle are equal.

A straight line and a circle cannot intersect in more than two points.

Two circles cannot intersect in more than two points.

In the same circle or in equal circles equal central angles have equal arcs.

In the same circle or in equal circles equal arcs have equal central angles.

The intersection of a plane and a sphere is a circle.

It is possible to construct an angle equal to any given angle.

If both terms of a ratio are multiplied or divided by the same number except 0, the ratio thus formed is equal to the original ratio.

The area of a rectangle is equal to the product of its base and altitude.

If two angles of one triangle are respectively equal to two angles of a second triangle, the two triangles are similar.

If an angle of one triangle equals an angle of a second triangle and the sides which include those angles are proportional, then the triangles are similar.

If the sides of one triangle are respectively proportional to the sides of a second triangle, then the triangles are similar.

All regular polygons which have the same number of sides are similar.

All of these assumptions were obtained by a continuation of those methods illustrated in Chapter III and are the result of group thinking. The great majority of them were recognized as implicit in conclusions reached and were then stated explicitly. The way in which the assumption "It is possible to draw one and only one line bisecting an angle" was derived, as discussed on page 65, is a good illustration of this. Others, however, such as "Vertical dihedral angles are equal," were recognized and suggested by the pupils, although they had no apparent connection with any conclusion already established. The statements, as given here, are in the form finally accepted by all pupils.

In the preceding chapter reference was made to "a small number of theorems which constitute a common background for all pupils and which serve as illustrations of what proof really means." The attention of *all* pupils was directed toward the discovery of these theorems through assumptions selected with this purpose in mind. Numerous illustrations showing how this was done are outlined in Chapter III, such as that on page 57 which deals with the theorem concerning the sum of the two interior angles on the same side of a transversal which intersects two parallel lines and also that on pages 58–60 by which the thinking of the pupils was directed toward the sum of the interior angles of a triangle. Other illustrations, showing only the suggestions which were given to the pupils, follow:

By your own definition "A parallelogram is a four sided figure with its opposite sides parallel." These properties which you have given to a parallelogram in this definition imply other properties. How many of these can you establish by deductive proof?

Referring to the diagram at the right let us assume that AP and AQ are tangents drawn to circle O from an external point, A. What are the implications of this assumption?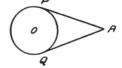

Draw a right triangle and from the vertex of the right angle draw a perpendicular to the hypotenuse. What properties of this figure can you discover and establish by deductive proof?

Through such suggestions as these the spirit of discovery was encouraged, important theorems were established, and the pupil gained an increasing appreciation of "what proof really means." In one case the individual forms the hypothesis that two line segments are equal, as in the second of the preceding illustrations. In another, he sets up the hypothesis that two angles are equal, or that two triangles are similar or whatever his considered judgment may suggest. Then he attempts to validate these hypotheses by logical proof, using whatever methods are available for this purpose. Once a conclusion has been thus established for a particular diagram he generalizes, and by such a process the following theorems were established by *all* pupils:

1. If a transversal cuts two parallel lines, then the alternate interior angles thus formed are equal.

2. If two lines are cut by a transversal and the alternate interior angles are equal, then the lines are parallel.

3. If a transversal cuts two parallel lines, then the interior angles on the same side of the transversal are supplementary.

4. The sum of the interior angles of any triangle is 180°.

5. The sum of the interior angles of any polygon is $(n - 2)$ 180°.

6. The sum of the exterior angles of any polygon is 360°.

7. In any isosceles triangle the angles opposite the equal sides are equal.

8. If the hypotenuse and a side of a right triangle are equal respectively to the hypotenuse and a side of another right triangle, then the two triangles are congruent.

9. The opposite angles of a parallelogram are equal.

10. The opposite sides of a parallelogram are equal.

11. If the opposite sides of a quadrilateral are equal, then the quadrilateral is a parallelogram.

12. If the diameter of a circle is perpendicular to a chord, then it bisects the chord and the two arcs formed by the chord.

13. If a line bisects a chord and is also perpendicular to the chord, then the line goes through the center of the circle.

14. An angle which is inscribed in a circle is measured by one half its intercepted arc.

15. A tangent of a circle is perpendicular to the radius drawn from the center of the circle to the point of tangency.

16. The tangents drawn from a given point to a circle are equal. The line drawn from the given point to the center of the circle is perpendicular to and bisects the line connecting the two points of tangency and bisects the angle formed by the tangents.

17. If two chords of a circle intersect, the product of the segments of one chord equals the product of the segments of the other chord.

18. If an altitude is drawn to the hypotenuse of a right triangle, the two triangles thus formed are similar to each other and each of them is similar to the given right triangle.

19. If an altitude is drawn to the hypotenuse of a right triangle, this altitude is a mean proportional to the two segments into which it divides the hypotenuse.

20. If an altitude is drawn to the hypotenuse of a right triangle, either of the arms is a mean proportional to the whole hypotenuse and the adjacent segment of the hypotenuse.

21. In any right triangle the sum of the squares on the two sides equals the square on the hypotenuse.

Among the assumptions made by the pupils were some which stated that it was possible to make certain constructions, and the teacher directed the attention of the pupils to the solution of these problems. For example, if "it is possible to construct an angle equal to a given angle," how can this be done? If "a line segment can be bisected by one and only one point," how may this point be determined? By raising such questions, the following problems were solved:

1. Bisect a given angle.
2. Bisect a given line segment.
3. Through a given point construct a perpendicular to a given line.
4. Construct an angle equal to a given angle.
5. Through a given point not on a given line draw a line parallel to a given line.

In addition to these theorems and problems which constituted a common background for all pupils, a number of other theorems were established from a study of the assumptions suggested in the "mimeographed material available to all students but not required of any." Pupils do not all work at the same rate and this "extra" material was provided for those who were interested to investigate further the assumptions which had been generally accepted. Even those pupils who worked most slowly had sufficient time to examine some of these assumptions and were successful in recognizing some of the less complex implications. A small group of pupils became interested in "inequalities" through their study of the isosceles triangle, and in their attempt to establish the relation between angles that were opposite unequal sides found that they needed assumptions which had not already been accepted. They stated these assumptions explicitly, placed them in their text, and proved the theorem that "if two sides of a triangle are unequal, then the angle opposite the larger side is greater than the angle opposite the smaller side."

It is well to emphasize again the fact that all of this individual work was done during the supervised study periods under the direction of the teacher. Guidance was given wherever it was needed. Pertinent questions were raised with individual pupils, helpful suggestions were made and the thinking of the pupil was thus directed toward the discovery of implications. The extent of this guidance varied with the pupil, but in no case was a complete proof given or even suggested. The spirit of discovery was encouraged and the pupil was expected to generalize any conclusion established for a particular diagram. The additional theorems thus established are given in Table 8 and the number of pupils proving each theorem is also indicated.

TABLE 8

ADDITIONAL THEOREMS ESTABLISHED BY THE PUPILS

Statement of Theorem	Number of Pupils Proving Theorem
If each of two lines is perpendicular to a transversal, then the two lines are parallel.	25
If a transversal cuts two lines in such a way that the two interior angles on the same side of the transversal are supplementary, then the two lines are parallel.	25
If a transversal cuts two parallel lines and if it is perpendicular to one of them, it is also perpendicular to the other.	25
If the arms of a right triangle are equal respectively to the arms of another right triangle, then the triangles are congruent.	25
The two acute angles of a right triangle are complementary.	23
If an angle is inscribed in a semicircle, then it is a right angle.	19
If two triangles are similar to the same triangle, then they are similar to each other.	18
If two angles of a triangle are equal, then the sides opposite these angles are equal.	16
The diagonals of a parallelogram bisect each other.	15
In any isosceles triangle the line bisecting the vertical angle also bisects the base and is perpendicular to the base.	14
If two angles have their sides respectively parallel, then they are either equal or supplementary.	12
An exterior angle of a triangle is equal to the sum of the two opposite interior angles.	10
If two angles of one triangle are equal respectively to the corresponding angles of a second triangle, then the third angles are equal.	10
If two angles and any side of one triangle are equal respectively to two angles and the corresponding side of another, then the triangles are congruent.	9

TABLE 8 (*Continued*)

ADDITIONAL THEOREMS ESTABLISHED BY THE PUPILS

Statement of Theorem	Number of Pupils Proving Theorem
If the diagonals of a quadrilateral bisect each other, then the quadrilateral is a parallelogram.	9
If two lines are parallel to a third line, then they are parallel to each other.	8
The area of a parallelogram is the product of the base and the height.	8
The size of each interior angle of a regular n-gon is $180°-360°/n$.	7
If two sides of a triangle are unequal, then the angle opposite the larger side is greater than the angle opposite the smaller side.	7
If two angles of a triangle are unequal, then the side opposite the larger angle is greater than the side opposite the smaller angle.	7
If the opposite angles of a quadrilateral are equal, then the quadrilateral is a parallelogram.	6
The area of any triangle is one-half the product of the base and corresponding height.	6
The angle between two chords of a circle is measured by one-half the sum of the intercepted arcs.	5
The angle between two intersecting secants is measured by one-half the difference of the intercepted arcs.	5
The angle between a secant and a tangent to a circle is measured by one-half the difference of the intercepted arcs.	5
The angle formed by two tangents to a circle is measured by one-half the difference between its intercepted arcs.	5
If a perpendicular is drawn from any one point on a circle to a diameter, this perpendicular is a mean proportional between the segments into which it divides the diameter.	5
The angle formed by a tangent and a chord drawn from the point of tangency is measured by one-half the included arc.	5
The area of a trapezoid is one-half the height times the sum of the two parallel sides.	4
If two angles have their sides respectively perpendicular, the angles are either equal or supplementary.	3
If a series of parallel lines cuts equal segments on one transversal, they cut equal segments on all other transversals.	3
The ratio of the area of any two similar triangles is the square of the ratio of similitude.	3
If from a point outside a circle a tangent and a secant are drawn, the tangent is the mean proportional between the secant and its external segment.	3

The additional problems that were solved by the pupils are given in Table 9.

TABLE 9

ADDITIONAL PROBLEMS SOLVED BY THE PUPILS

Statement of Problem	Number of Pupils Solving Problem
At a given point on a circle construct a tangent to the circle.	20
Given two line segments, construct the mean proportional between them.	5
Through a given point outside a circle draw a tangent to the circle.	4
Construct a triangle with its three sides equal respectively to three given line segments.	3
Construct a triangle having given two sides and the included angle.	3
Construct a triangle having given two angles and the included side.	3

The concept of "locus" was considered as the "place of all points which met certain given conditions." This concept was extended to include three dimensions and, although no proofs were given, the following propositions were stated and accepted by the pupils:

The locus of all points in a plane equidistant from two given points is the perpendicular bisector of the straight line joining the two points.

The locus of all points in three-dimensional space equidistant from two given points is the plane which is perpendicular to the line joining these two points and passing through the midpoint of this line.

The locus of all points equidistant from two intersecting lines is the pair of lines which bisect the angles formed by the two intersecting lines.

The locus of all points equidistant from two intersecting planes is the pair of planes which bisect the dihedral angles formed by the two intersecting planes.

The locus of all points in a plane at a given distance from a given line consists of two lines parallel to the given line and at the given distance from it, one being on one side of the line and one being on the other side.

The locus of all points in three-dimensional space at a given distance from a given line is a cylindric surface whose axis is the given line and whose radius is the given distance.

The locus of all points in three-dimensional space at a given distance from a given plane consists of two planes parallel to the given plane and at the given distance from it, one being on one side of the plane and one being on the other side.

The locus of all points in a plane at a given distance from a given point is a circle whose center is the given point and whose radius is the given distance.

The locus of all points in three-dimensional space at a given distance from a given point is a sphere whose center is the given point and whose radius is the given distance.

Just as the concept of locus was extended to three dimensions other concepts were similarly extended. The lines, planes and dihedral angles in the room in which the pupils worked were used as illustrations of three-dimensional ideas, and through a continuation of the procedures outlined in Chapter III the following propositions, usually recognized as theorems to be proved in a regular solid geometry course, were accepted:

If two planes intersect, they can intersect in one and only one line.

If a plane intersects two parallel planes, then the alternate dihedral angles thus formed are equal.

If two planes intersect in such a manner that the adjacent dihedral angles are equal, then the two planes are perpendicular.

An infinite number of perpendiculars can be drawn to a given line at any given point on the line and these perpendiculars all lie in the plane perpendicular to the given line through the given point.

Through a given point not on a given plane it is possible to pass one and only one plane parallel to the given plane.

Through a given point there is one and only one line perpendicular to a given plane.

Through a given point there is one and only one plane perpendicular to a given line.

If two parallel planes are intersected by another plane, then the lines of intersection are parallel.

If two lines are parallel and a plane is passed through one and only one of these lines, it is parallel to the other line.

If two lines are each perpendicular to the same plane, then they are parallel to each other.

If two planes are each perpendicular to the same line, then they are parallel to each other.

If each of two intersecting planes is perpendicular to a third plane, then the intersection of these planes is also perpendicular to the third plane.

If each of two intersecting lines is parallel to a plane, then the plane which these two intersecting lines determine is parallel to that plane.

In the judgment of the teacher these experiences of the pupils in selecting undefined terms, making definitions, accepting assumptions and searching for their implications served as an excellent preparation for a consideration of the ideas presented in Professor Keyser's book *Thinking about Thinking*. About the middle of the second year the pupils were introduced to this book through the discussion of certain selected portions read by the teacher. This aroused considerable interest and all pupils read Chapters II and IV while some of them read the entire book. The discussion[1] which followed revealed a comprehensive understanding of the ideas covered. Empirical and postulational thinking were contrasted and the long history of man's effort to find "the truth" was recognized as an important factor in the evolution of proof. There seemed to be a "readiness" on the part of the pupils for careful consideration of these ideas, and the teacher asked each of them to prepare a paper[2] on "The Evolution of Proof," giving careful attention to such points as:

The contribution of the Egyptians.

The contribution of the Greeks.

The "absolute truth" of Euclid's conclusions.

The contributions of such men as Saccheri, Lobatchewsky, Bolyai, and Riemann.

The modern concept of proof.

To assist in the preparation of this paper references were given to the following books:

Sanford, Vera. *A Short History of Mathematics*. Houghton, Mifflin Co., 1930.

Smith, David Eugene. *History of Mathematics*, Vol. 2, Ginn and Co., 1925.

Bell, Eric T. *The Search for Truth*. The Williams and Wilkins Co., 1934.

---

[1] Among the observers during this discussion were six seniors from the College of Education. Their observation reports, written for their college teachers, reveal their opinion as to the thinking of the pupils. Pertinent parts of these reports are given in the next chapter on "Evaluation."

[2] Samples of these papers are given in the Appendix.

Six pupils, however, did not limit themselves to these three books and an examination of the bibliographies they presented reveals that in addition the following references were used:

Encyclopedia Britannica. Vol. xxv, Logic and Proof.
Keyser, C. J. Thinking about Thinking. E. P. Dutton and Co., 1926.
Russell, Bertrand. Introduction to Mathematical Philosophy. Macmillan and Co., 1919.
Smith, David Eugene. Mathematics. Longmans, Green and Co., 1928.
Smith, David Eugene. A Source Book in Mathematics. McGraw Hill Book Co., 1929.

The pupils recognized that the preparation of this paper was related to their work in English, and they received helpful criticism and suggestions from the English teacher who accepted the papers as a part of the writing expected of each pupil.

In summarizing the activities of these pupils it should again be pointed out that the class met four times each week for periods of forty minutes. No pupil was expected to do any work outside of class, and provision was made within class time for all needed study which meant that this time was used for the following purposes:

1. *Periods for general discussion and group guidance*

These periods afforded opportunity for the interplay of minds and helped to establish the background common to the experience of all pupils. Conclusions already established were analyzed, questions were raised through which attention was directed toward the discovery of "new" theorems and opportunity was afforded for each pupil to contribute to the thinking of the group concerning the points under discussion. Tangible outcomes were found in the general agreements reached as to:

a. The selection of the undefined terms.
b. The terms to be defined and their accepted definitions.
c. The recognition and explicit statement of assumptions.

These periods also provided opportunity for discussing certain phases of the history of mathematics, for a consideration of such books as *Thinking about Thinking, The Search for*

Truth and for a study of any material pertinent to the changing concept of what proof really means.

2. *Periods for supervised study and individual guidance*

A summary of the different sorts of activities carried on during these periods follows:

- a. Planning the organization of the textbook and keeping the development of this book up to date. (Required of all pupils)
- b. Analysis of arguments presented in non-mathematical material. (Required of all pupils)
- c. Library reading related to the history of mathematics, the practical aspects of geometry, and the evolution of proof. (Required of all pupils)
- d. Examining the implications of assumptions suggested in mimeographed material. (Not required of any pupils)

Each pupil was free to use these periods of supervised study on any of the above activities which for one reason or another claimed his attention. The teacher was free to confer with each pupil and made a definite point of helping those who, in his judgment, needed guidance in directing their own activity. Whenever it seemed advisable, individual conferences outside of class time were arranged.

The ratio of the time spent in general discussion to that spent in supervised study varied considerably with the development of the work. During the first three months this ratio was approximately 3 : 1, while for the last six months it was approximately 1 : 3. As the pupils became more familiar with postulational thinking and the nature of proof, they needed more time for independent investigation, and this ratio for the entire course was approximately 1 : 2.

CHAPTER V

EVALUATION

DIFFERENT KINDS OF EVALUATION

NUMEROUS tests are available by which the mathematical facts memorized and the skills acquired as a result of the procedures outlined in Chapter III can be measured. To make such an evaluation is a comparatively easy task but for purposes of this study it is relatively unimportant. Our major concern is to determine as nearly as possible the effect of this sort of training on the behavior of the pupils and the extent to which their reflective thinking has been improved. There is no one way by which such an evaluation can be made. While paper-and-pencil tests may reveal potentialities for the behavior defined on pages 11–12 they cannot guarantee that the actual behavior of the pupils is consistent with the results indicated. In discussing this problem, Dr. Ralph W. Tyler says that "All methods of evaluating human behavior involve four technical problems: defining the behavior to be evaluated, determining the situations in which it is expressed, developing a record of the behavior which takes place in these situations, and evaluating the recorded behavior."[1] In a later article where he further discusses this problem, Tyler writes, "An adequate evaluation involves the collection of appropriate evidence as to the changes taking place in pupils in the various directions which are important for educational development. This evidence is not limited to that obtained from paper-and-pencil examinations. It may include records of observations of young people, the collection of products of their work . . . and evidences regarding the purposes which progressive schools are attempting to realize."[2] The sources of data used for this evaluation are:

[1] Ralph W. Tyler, "Techniques for Evaluating Behavior," *Educational Research Bulletin*, Ohio State University, Vol. xiii, No. 1, 1934, pp. 1–2.

[2] Ralph W. Tyler, "Evaluation: a Challenge to Progressive Education," *Educational Research Bulletin*, Vol. xiv, No. 1, 1935, pp. 9–16.

1. Record of scores made by pupils on the Ohio Every Pupil Test in plane geometry.
2. Results of paper-and-pencil tests on the nature of proof applied to non-mathematical situations.
3. Contributions of students illustrating situations to which habits of thought developed in their study of the nature of proof had transferred.
4. Parents' observations concerning improvement in the critical thinking of their child.
5. Record of six observations made by college seniors.
6. Students' observations concerning improvement in their ability to think critically.

THE OHIO EVERY PUPIL TEST

While the control of geometric subject matter was not one of the major purposes to be accomplished by the pupils in Class A, nevertheless it seemed desirable to compare their achievement in this respect with that of pupils who had followed the usual course in geometry. The April, 1936, Ohio Every Pupil Test in plane geometry[3] was used for this purpose. The highest possible score was 80, and the scores of the 2,772 pupils who took this test ranged from 2.0 to 79.0 while the scores of the pupils in Class A ranged from 15.0 to 79.0. The median score of the pupils throughout the state was 36.5, while the median score of the pupils in Class A was 52.0, this score falling between the 80th and 90th percentiles of the state scores.

These results would seem to indicate that even though the pupils in Class A had covered only a small part of the geometric content usually studied in plane geometry they knew at least as much about those aspects of the subject which this test measures as the larger group throughout the state. In general, they found the test too long to be completed within the 45 minutes allowed and a number stated that if the time had been longer they could have worked out many of the results which, in view of their limited acquaintance with the subject matter, were entirely new to them. It is probably safe to say that the constant emphasis on method at the expense of content had decreased the content familiar to

[3] A copy of this test may be found in the Appendix.

them but had increased their power of attack on new and original exercises. At any rate, there seems to have been no loss in control of subject matter.

"NATURE OF PROOF" TEST

At the beginning of the year a pre-test[4] on the nature of proof applied to non-mathematical material was given to each of four different classes. Two of these were Class A and Class B, described on pages 19–20 of Chapter II. The other two classes, which were in two different schools, will be called Class C and Class D. Each was a tenth grade class in plane geometry. In Class C there were 34 pupils and in Class D there were 25 pupils. Classes B, C and D followed the usual formal course in demonstrative geometry. Class A was used for the experimental work, and the program of the fifty pupils in Classes A and B differed with respect to each other only in regard to the geometry, while they differed in many ways from the programs of Classes C and D.

TABLE 10

CHANGE IN ABILITY TO ANALYZE NON-MATHEMATICAL
MATERIAL AFTER ONE YEAR'S STUDY OF GEOMETRY

| CLASS | MEAN SCORES | | | | | |
	Pre-Test	S.E.	Final Test	S.E.	Change	S.E.
A	16.7	0.9	24.2	0.8	7.5	1.2
B	13.0	0.9	14.0	0.7	1.0	1.1
C	14.3	0.5	14.1	0.6	−0.2	0.8
D	13.8	0.8	12.3	0.6	−1.5	1.0
B, C, D	13.8	0.4	13.5	0.4	−0.3	0.6

At the end of the year Classes C and D had completed all required work in geometry whereas Classes A and B had completed only the first half of their work in accordance with the conditions outlined on pages 21–22. This test was again given at this time to each of the four groups. Four different people, one of whom was the writer, scored these tests independently and from the results a composite score was found for each pupil. The mean scores for each class and also for

[4] Refer to Appendix for a copy of this test.

Classes B, C and D combined are given in Table 10, page 103.

The pre-test was actually given three weeks after the opening of the school year. During this time much emphasis was placed on the importance of definition in Class A, and this doubtless had some effect on the pre-test score in this class. However, it will be noted that the ability of the pupils in Class A to handle material of the sort given in the test definitely improved during the year, while there was no change of any importance in the classes where formal demonstrative geometry was taught.

Since the programs of the pupils in Classes A and B were alike with the exception of the work in geometry, it seemed profitable to compare further the results of these two groups. Three criteria were selected. Criterion P is improvement in ability to analyze material of the sort in the nature of proof test. Criterion Q is the amount of retention of this ability at the end of the summer vacation. Criterion R is achievement in respect to the traditional objectives of geometry. At the end of the first year the pupils in both classes took the same test[5] in formal geometry and these scores were available. Scores on retention were also available for both groups. The procedure here followed consists in using the known factors in one of the groups for the purpose of predicting outcomes in the other group. Regression equations were developed and in this particular case these equations were as follows:

$$X_P = .139 \, X_1 + .281 \, X_2 + 2.46$$
$$X_Q = .319 \, X_1 + .284 \, X_2 - 7.32$$
$$X_R = 2.44 \, X_1 + .235 \, X_2 - 147.12$$

where 1 represents the Otis intelligence score and 2 represents the pre-test score on the nature of proof. These equations are based entirely on the achievement made in Class A, while Class B has not been utilized in any way, and they can thus be used to predict the expected achievement in Class B had the teaching procedures for this group been the same as

[5] Refer to the Appendix for a copy of this test.

those used in Class A. The results are given in Table 11 and in each case the predicted achievement is higher than the actual achievement, which suggests that the procedures used in Class A yielded more effective results. There is, however, the possibility that these differences in achievement may be

TABLE 11

ACTUAL AND PREDICTED ACHIEVEMENT IN CLASS B

Criterion	Actual Achievement of Class B	Predicted Achievement of Class B	Difference* S. E.
P (non-mathematical material)	13.98	22.36	13.97
Q (Retention)	25.45	32.62	7.17
R (Geometric Proofs)	84.83	127.55	6.74

*These values were determined by the formula:

$$\frac{\text{difference}}{\dfrac{\sigma\sqrt{1-R^2}}{\sqrt{N-1}}}$$

where R is the multiple correlation of how well criterion scores can be predicted in Class B.

due to factors which were uncontrolled, but they cannot be due to pupil variations in the Otis intelligence scores or in the pre-test scores in the nature of proof.

ILLUSTRATIONS OF TRANSFER

The results of the paper-and-pencil tests on the nature of proof suggest that the pupils in Class A had "potentialities for the kind of behavior defined on pages 11–12," but evidence is needed as to whether or not these habits of thought were actually used outside the classroom. One kind of evidence is found in the pupils' voluntary contributions which illustrate situations to which these habits of thought did actually transfer. Table 12 gives illustrations of transfer contributed by pupils.

TABLE 12

ILLUSTRATIONS OF TRANSFER CONTRIBUTED BY PUPILS

Nature of Contribution	Number of Such Contributions	Different Pupils Making This Kind of Contribution
Analysis of current advertisements	13	9
Illustrations where discussion was clarified by pointing out conflicts in definition	Other classes 11	9
	Out of school 5	4
Analysis of editorials, magazine and newspaper articles	9	7
Recognition of unexpressed implications in non-mathematical data	3	3
Analysis of lectures and ministers' sermons	2	2
Analysis of political material	2	2
How exposition has been clarified	2	2
How important decisions have been reached through careful examination of evidence	2	2

Of the twenty-five pupils in Class A, twenty of them contributed one or more illustrations of this sort. It should be emphasized that these contributions were entirely voluntary. These twenty pupils recognized that their reflective thinking had been improved through their study of proof and they were sufficiently interested to record these illustrations of transfer. This does not mean that these were the only illustrations available nor does it mean that the other five pupils had nothing of this sort to contribute. It simply means that no other illustrations of this kind were recorded. There is perhaps some significance to the fact that most of these contributions were made during the second year.

OBSERVATIONS OF PARENTS

While the contributions listed in Table 12 were made voluntarily, there is a possibility that the influence of the teacher may have been a factor in this situation since these contributions were given to him for his examination. In an effort to learn whether or not there had been any change in the critical thinking of these pupils in situations entirely removed from the influence of the teacher, the parents were interviewed individually. It was neither possible nor advisable for the teacher to conduct these interviews, and the man selected for this purpose was an experienced mathematics teacher who had visited the class, knew something of the nature of the work, and had expressed mild doubt as to its value. These interviews occurred during the latter part of the second year when the course was nearing completion. The parents knew nothing of this work from firsthand contact with it. Their judgment of its value was determined by the reaction of their child and their observation of its effect on his thinking. Through informal discussion with the individual parents, supplemented by direct questions when advisable, the interviewer secured a record of ways in which the parents believed this work had improved the critical thinking of their child. It was possible to see the parents of only twenty-two of the pupils. A summary of the comments obtained through such interviews is given in Table 13.

TABLE 13

OBSERVATIONS OF PARENTS CONCERNING CHANGES IN PUPILS

Kind of Comment Made by 22 Parents		Number Making Comment
Attitude toward formal geometry	Formal geometry course is a waste of time.	15
	Any change in formal geometry would be an improvement.	3
	Formal geometry develops logical thinking but improvement in method is needed.	3
Pupil's interest in course	Very enthusiastic about the course.	19
	Moderately interested in the course.	2
	Dislikes the course.	1

TABLE 13 (*Continued*)

OBSERVATIONS OF PARENTS CONCERNING CHANGES IN PUPILS

Kind of Comment Make by 22 Parents		Number Making Comment
Cause for pupil's attitude toward course	Child believes course has taught him how to think.	9
	Child enjoys all phases of mathematics.	2
	Child says he has wasted his time in the course.	1
Parent's judgment on value of course	The course has been of real value to my child.	17
	The most profitable course my child has ever taken.	13
	Doubts preparation of child for college mathematics.	2
Parent's judgment as to effect of course on child	The course has definitely improved the ability of my child to think critically.	16
	Through this course my child has learned to like mathematics.	3
	The course has improved my child's power of concentration.	1
Parents giving one or more illustrations of critical thinking definitely attributed to the work of the course.		13

The illustrations supplied by the parents were not fundamentally different from those given in Table 12, although they covered a wider range of activity. In addition to an analysis of advertisements, magazine articles, editorials, political speeches, and sermons were such illustrations as:

"Recognition of hidden assumptions underlying church doctrines."

"More effective and wiser use of money."

"Questioning of assumptions on which choice of profession was based."

"Recognition of false assumptions in speech on foreign relations."

"Entering more freely into adult conversation because of added insight."

"Helping to remove child's prejudices."

Some parents, even though they considered the course valuable, felt that it might tend to make their child too critical and encourage quibbling. All quotations of this sort are taken in full from the report of the interviewer:

> "The mother thinks that the girl has become too cynical and is given to a great amount of quibbling."

> "The parents fear that the course may tend to inhibit in the boy the power of imagination for creative writing in English. For example, when he was writing of a personal experience for an English assignment he resented some suggestions his mother made in order to add interest to the composition on the basis that the suggestions were not facts. He wished to write only in a scientific manner."

> "The mother fears that the girl may carry her criticism to the point of quibbling, however. In some cases she has gone to the point of criticising authorities on subjects about which she knew nothing."

While various interpretations might be given to the significance of these three quotations there seems to be no question concerning the fact of transfer. The parents appear to believe that through this course the thinking of their children has become more critical, and their only concern is that it should not become too critical. The probability is that work of this sort will tend to reduce "quibbling," for it should enable the student to focus his attention on the critical and fundamental points in any discussion.

REPORTS OF OBSERVERS

Among the many observers who visited the class were a number of mathematics seniors from the college of education. They were required to write reports of their observation and these reports were given to their college teachers. They were not written for the classroom teacher nor did the observers have any idea they would be seen by him. Some of them, however, did fall into his hands, and the following pertinent quotations are taken from six different papers:

1. "The students were working, each at his own problem while the teacher discussed points with each of them and raised questions concerning relations which they had missed. The motivation of those students must have been particularly forceful for, even though they were working on at least four different types of material, there was *very* little wasted time. One of the methods of motivating these students seemed especially interesting to me. In the written work which the pupils had just handed in they had considered the problem of defining 'restaurant' in connection with an industrial code which had come up before the legis-

lature. Adults were struggling to find a definition which would include the business houses desired. That these students should tackle this situation, which had been made meaningful and interesting to them through this course, and that they were able to analyze the situation and point out specific difficulties made the assignment interesting. I particularly liked that plan used in this classroom situation in which the students work at their own speed, putting in extra time where they need it or on parts in which they are interested but are kept as a group by the group discussions of work that all students have completed or ideas which are new to all of them."

2. "On this particular day there was no group work or class discussion. The pupils were working individually on different problems. The teacher, however, showed me some of the materials of the course which gave me a much clearer understanding of it. This included some work on the A.A.A. referendum, some political statements and some statements of newspaper policy. I was amazed at the intelligence and clear thinking that the students did on these problems. One knew just exactly where they stood and what their position meant. They pointed out definitely the assumptions on which the writers based their conclusions. (I am inclined to think that the writers of the original statements did not realize their basic assumptions.) The pupils further pointed out words which the writers had failed to define and showed unusual ability in clear, logical thinking.

"I also had the privilege of examining some papers which the students had handed in voluntarily. These papers dealt with more or less the same type of thing and ranged in length from one paragraph to several pages. One very short one showed that an argument in a psychology class was definitely settled when the protagonists agreed on their definition of 'genius.' Another criticized some loose thinking in the Reader's Digest; another tore an advertisement to pieces.

"In summary, I could tell that the pupils were receiving a very definite practical kind of geometry; that they were being trained in autonomous thinking of the highest type."

3. "After listening to the class discussion I felt that I understood much better than before the material in the book 'Thinking about Thinking' and I am sure that the students themselves understood the material better than before. Not one of the students seemed to feel that the material in the text was dry and uninteresting and I really feel that the book was more difficult than most books with which high school students have to deal. There was a keen interest in the recitation and a respect for the other person's opinion manifested in the classroom. Altogether, the hour spent was a profitable one and I am sure that each person who heard the discussion is a more intelligent person than before."

4. "The discussion for the day was based on Keyser's book, 'Thinking about Thinking.' I was particularly impressed by the active participation of the students in the discussion. They did the discussing, made

suggestions and took exception to points brought up. The teacher had very little talking to do and yet the situation was one in which the students were very interested, were thinking on the subject and were really learning to think.

"I believe that the ease with which those children took exception to the teacher's ideas emphasizes the novel relationship which exists between teacher and pupil in that school situation. It might also be considered an index to the amount and kind of thinking done by the child. The intelligence of the questions asked by those students far surpassed that found in the ordinary high school situation."

5. "The class pointed out that autonomous thinking was of the 'if-then' type, involving undefined terms, defined terms, assumptions and finally conclusions. They gave an excellent illustration of autonomous thinking with 3 + 4 = 7 as an example, listing the definitions and assumptions involved in this reasoning. Throughout the discussion they showed an unusual familiarity with other number systems as well as historic contributions to mathematics and they demonstrated their capability in thinking in terms of number systems other than our own. They questioned statements of each other and of the teacher. There was nothing sloppy or slip-shod in their thinking.

"This observation, together with previous ones I have made of the same class, has convinced me of the value that can be derived from high school mathematics. I have often doubted the justifiability of much of it and I feel that I, myself, derived very little practical benefit from my high school mathematics courses. However, I am now armed with equipment that will answer attacks on the place of mathematics in school. I believe that I can make it fill a definite need for I wonder if many a veteran mathematics teacher wouldn't have felt himself unequal to the pupils in this class during that discussion. Those pupils showed that they had a method of thinking that would apply to all fields of thought."

6. "The pupils discussed Keyser's 'Thinking about Thinking' and the particular class which I observed was devoted to a comprehensive consideration of the book. It seemed quite remarkable that the individual members of the class independently anticipated Keyser's steps outlined in the process of thinking. These steps were expressed in an original manner and were arrived at usually by intelligent and thoughtful questions. Only after the pupils had formulated definite thoughts on the steps of thinking were their ideas verified by direct quotations from Keyser.

"Such pertinent ideas as 'No one does only autonomous thinking,' 'The simplest habit formation at the outset was autonomous thinking' and the like were brought out by members of the class and were immediately met with active thought and discussion on the part of the rest of the members of the class. Mathematics history was not neglected in the class discussion and such names as Euclid, Saccheri, Bolyai and Lobatchewsky were commonly used by the pupils."

While these quotations give no detailed evaluation of the pupils' progress, they do present a picture of the class from six different points of view and give some evidence as to the judgment of these mathematics majors concerning the quality of thinking done by the pupils.

EVALUATION BY PUPILS

All pupils in the school were encouraged to evaluate their own progress, and many of those in Class A wrote statements concerning values which they felt they had derived from their experiences in this class. While the writer is conscious of the limitations of these statements for purposes of evaluation, they do reveal a point of view considerably different from that expressed by the pupils before the work began. One has only to contrast these statements with those given in the table on page 29 to realize that a definite change occurred in the judgment of the pupils as to the value of this work. Only eighteen of the pupils were inclined to make this written evaluation. Their individual statements follow:

1. "I can truthfully say that my course in geometry has meant more to me than any course in my eleven years of school. At the beginning of the year I dreaded the thought of geometry, but now I wouldn't have missed the course for anything. It has changed my whole line of thinking. Before this year I had always taken everything the people said for granted without examining it, but now I am able to think critically and to analyze statements, and I find myself doing this unconsciously. I am much more able to think clearly. I think this course in geometry should be an absolute requirement in every school for I am convinced that after that people would be more conscious of using language loosely, and that their critical attitude would end a lot of fraud in advertising and in politics."

2. "This year's work in geometry has had more effect on what I have done and thought outside of school than any other class this year. It has made me critical of things I read and hear that I have never noticed before. It has made me critical of the statements I make and the things I do."

3. "I feel that my work in geometry and the nature of proof has been one of the most valuable experiences and also one of the most enjoyable experiences that I have had during my school experiences. I feel this way because the work I have done has made an impression upon my brain which will affect and aid all aspects of my life. By learning to think clearly and express myself clearly I will be able to use the time that is given to me in my life to its best advantage."

4. "Perhaps during this year I have shown no great intelligence, or to the contrary, the lack of it. On my brain has been made one of the deepest impressions it has ever received. Before this course the word 'analysis' held no deeper or finer meaning—it was just a word that I had used but it really meant nothing. My thinking has become more calm, although not calm enough. Now I notice sentences and think about their significance. I could see the basic assumptions behind statements before I took geometry, but now I am more able to see them clearly."

5. "I have never in my whole school life in mathematics spent a more profitable year. I have not only learned how to prove theorems but also to think critically and analytically about everything in my life. If I had just taken a course in plane geometry I believe that when I was finished with it I would forget most of it as I don't plan to teach it or use it in any such way. But in this class I have learned things that I will never forget and will use in all areas all my life. This has been an invaluable experience and any student beginning geometry will certainly profit, in my opinion, by a similar experience."

6. "At the first of this year I rather dreaded the thought of taking geometry, but now I am very, very glad I did. It has helped me, first, in that I am more careful of the statements I make. The wording has become more important to me. Secondly, I have learned to pick flaws in other people's arguments and statements, which I have always felt hopelessly incapable of. I have never before in my life enjoyed mathematics as I have this year. I don't know how much geometry I learned but I do know I learned what assumptions and definitions mean in the world around me, and what a real proof is."

7. "I feel this year's work in geometry has made more impression on me than any year of mathematics I have had thus far. The reason I think so is that the work has been very interesting, and I have learned to go into detail and to say what I mean instead of just using language."

8. "I have learned to use logical thinking to a much greater degree than formerly. However, I think that you made a mistake in not mentioning the fundamental assumption on which logic rests, i.e. if you start with true assumptions and definitions, with correct logic you must reach a true conclusion. That assumption appears self evident; but there are many false statements which also appear that way."

9. "The course in geometry is the first mathematics that I have ever liked. I have found much pleasure in geometry. At times the work seemed to go ahead slowly, but on looking back I attribute that to my impatience. This course has made me a keen listener. It has taught me to pick little imperfections in reasoning which I would never have noticed otherwise. It has afforded a good chance to try to conquer my impatient attitude and above all it has taught me to reason well and not set up a plan that leaked like a sieve. It has also taught me to try to look through to a conclusion. I think this course valuable, not

because of the geometry as such, but the geometry as stressed here will be a most valuable contribution to my life."

10. "This year's geometry class has changed my way of thinking more than any other influence in my life. I am not just accepting things now unless their definitions and assumptions coincide more or less with mine. Previous to this time I don't believe I really thought seriously enough about a certain subject or other. Mathematics has never been made very interesting to me, and therefore I never cared much about the study, but this year's course was most interesting and it has made me see the connection and bearing upon my own life."

11. "This course in geometry is the first of its kind that I have ever taken or ever imagined. Never have I ever been instructed in the use of pure reasoning that it has given me. I find myself looking at problems in life differently because of my knowledge of pure thinking than I did before I started my geometry. In the skills of geometry I feel that our class is as well prepared as any class in the city schools which memorizes the proof of propositions."

12. "I feel that this year's work in geometry has helped me to analyze other phases of work. It has made me criticize things more thoroughly. I have always enjoyed my mathematics work and this year has been especially interesting. I have recognized the looseness of our language and I hope I have improved in my use of it."

13. "The work in geometry has helped me a lot in other fields. I simply delight in analyzing statements made by my friends, and advertisements. I've enjoyed this year of geometry more than any other year of mathematics. This class has changed my whole method of thinking out problems, and I'm not likely to forget it."

14. "This year I came to school expecting to hate geometry but happily my expectations weren't fulfilled. This year's work in geometry has made my powers to reason much better. I have learned to go behind statements and pick out the assumptions and to draw true conclusions. The words assumption, definition and conclusion have a new meaning to me. Whenever I hear them my mind jumps to this class. I can truthfully say that I have got more from this course than from any other course this year with the exception of French, although in French I've just learned facts. Now I'm more careful about what I can believe in a statement."

15. "I think I have begun to think things out more clearly since I have been taking this course. It has made me realize how loosely many arguments are constructed. The only thing I regret is that I don't think I have worked or thought hard enough on those things. It has helped me in other subjects too."

16. "I feel that I have accomplished more in this class this year than in any of my other classes. I used to hate any kind of mathematics. Since I have been here my interest has increased many fold. I feel that this year has been the best of all. Learning to do critical thinking

as we have been doing has, I think, done wonders for me. Nearly every time I read anything I unconsciously try to pick out assumptions behind it. Now when I read advertisements they seem so weak and sometimes I wonder why they never seemed so before. I have enjoyed coming to class and working here more than I thought I ever could. After hating mathematics as I used to and now liking it so, I feel that I have found something which has made and will make my life more full."

17. "Last year before school started, I used to think about geometry, and how so many people hated and dreaded the thought of taking it. To my great surprise I found it to be my most interesting period, and it wasn't because I am mathematically inclined, but rather, because of the way it was taught with reference to outside life. And now when I think about the many years that I had hardly known geometry existed, I wonder how I ever got along. I feel that this work in geometry has helped me so much, not only in making assumptions in school but also in conversing outside of school."

18. "This has been, I think, the most interesting study I have had this year. I know I got the most out of it for it has made me more critical of statements made by people and of advertisements. I liked the work in geometry very much and I wish there had been more of it. When you gave us statements to analyze for the assumptions on which they were based I don't think you should have counted off for an assumption you thought was not right. I don't see how you could because we all don't think as you do."

According to Dr. Ralph W. Tyler, "The first problem" in making this kind of an evaluation "is to get some evidence with reference to these so-called 'intangible' objectives. A later problem is to refine this evidence and make it more exact. There is no use to attack the second problem first. We cannot develop refined measures until we have first devised ways of collecting some objective evidence, even though they are crude. . . . By a careful study of boys and girls and a record of their behavior in a variety of situations, it is often possible to discover a few indicative situations in which one may get a clear picture of the development of that boy or girl without having to study him in all the possible situations of life."[6]

The writer frankly recognizes that this evaluation does not make use of conventional objective devices for measurement which some may consider desirable. It is, however, the result

[6] Ralph W. Tyler, *op. cit.*, p. 15.

of an honest effort to secure evidence concerning important outcomes which no standardized tests will measure, and it seems more valuable to secure some evidence, however crude, about outcomes that are important than to secure the most refined evidence about outcomes that are relatively unimportant.

CHAPTER VI

GENERAL SUMMARY

TEACHERS of mathematics agree, at least verbally, that the most important reason for teaching demonstrative geometry is to acquaint the pupils with certain ideas related to the nature of deductive proof and to make them familiar with postulational thinking as a general method of thought. While these purposes are generally recognized as valid from the standpoint of general education, there is serious question concerning the extent to which they are realized through the usual course in this subject. The theorems are not important in themselves. It is the *method* by which they are established that is important, and in this study geometric theorems are used only for the purpose of illustrating this method. The procedures used are derived from four basic assumptions:

1. That a senior high school student has reasoned and reasoned accurately before he begins the study of demonstrative geometry.
2. That he should have the opportunity to reason about the subject matter of geometry in his own way.
3. That the logical processes which should guide the development of the work should be those of the student and not those of the teacher.
4. That opportunity be provided for the application of the postulational method to non-mathematical material.

Non-mathematical situations of interest to the pupils were used to introduce them to the importance of definition and to the fact that conclusions depend on assumptions, many of which are often unrecognized. To make definitions and assumptions and to investigate their implications is to have firsthand experience with the method of mathematics. The concepts of space were accepted as the content with which these definitions and assumptions would deal, and the pupils were encouraged to think about this content in their own way.

In an effort to agree on the definition of certain concepts the necessity for undefined terms was recognized.

The following general procedures are implicit in the illustrations of Chapter III:

1. No general text was used. Each pupil developed his own text and was given the opportunity to develop it in his own way.
2. The undefined terms were selected by the pupils.
3. No attempt was made to reduce the number of undefined terms to a minimum.
4. The terms needing definition were selected by the pupils and the definitions were an outgrowth of the work rather than the basis for it.
5. Definitions were made by the pupils. Loose and ambiguous statements were refined and improved by criticisms and suggestions until they were accepted by all pupils.
6. Propositions which seemed obvious to the pupils were accepted as assumptions.
7. These assumptions were made by the pupils and were recognized by them as the product of their own thinking.
8. No attempt was made to reduce the number of assumptions to a minimum.
9. The detection of implicit or tacit assumptions was encouraged and recognized as important.
10. No statement of anything to be proved is given the pupil. Certain properties of a figure are assumed and the pupil is encouraged to discover the implications of these assumed properties.
11. No generalized statement is made before the pupil has had an opportunity to think about the implications of the particular properties assumed. This generalization is made by the pupil after he has himself discovered it.
12. Through the assumptions made the attention of all pupils is directed toward the discovery of a few theorems which seem important to the teacher.
13. Assumptions leading to theorems that are relatively unimportant are suggested in mimeographed material which is available to all pupils but not required of any.

14. Matters of common concern such as the selection of undefined terms, the making of definitions, the statement of assumptions and the generalizing of an implication are topics for general discussion while periods of supervised study provide for individual guidance.

15. The major emphasis is not on the theorems proved but rather on *the method of proof*. This method is generalized and applied to non-mathematical situations.

Illustrative exercises dealing with the analysis of non-mathematical material are given in Chapter III. Outcomes related to geometric content are given in Chapter IV; these outcomes vary with the individual pupil although all pupils had a common background of the twenty-one theorems given on page 92.

From the results of the evaluation it is probably safe to make the following generalizations:

1. Mathematical method illustrated by a small number of theorems yields a control of the subject matter of geometry at least equal to that obtained from the usual formal course.

2. By following the procedures outlined in Chapter III it is possible to improve the reflective thinking of secondary school pupils.

3. This improvement in the pupil's ability for reflective thinking is general in character and transfers to a variety of situations.

4. The usual formal course in demonstrative geometry does not improve the reflective thinking of the pupils.

PROBLEMS FOR FURTHER STUDY

It is the opinion of the writer that the study of proof should not be considered as a course which a pupil begins at a certain point in his secondary school experience and which he completes at the end of a given time. To encourage a pupil to think that he understands all there is to know about proof because he has had a "course" on that topic is to ignore the fact that even the most respected mathematicians disagree on what a proof is. There are, however, aspects of this important topic which the pupils in our secondary schools can understand and which, in the opinion of the writer, contribute effectively to the general education of these young people. The concept of proof is one concerning which the pupil should have a growing and increasing understanding. It is a concept which not only pervades his work in mathematics but is also involved in all situations where conclusions are to be reached and decisions to be made. Mathematics has a unique contribution to make in the development of this concept, and up to the present time teachers of mathematics have, in general, assumed that this contribution can best be made in the tenth year through the study of demonstrative geometry. The practice resulting from this assumption has tended to isolate the concept of proof, whereas this concept may well serve to unify the mathematical experiences of the pupil. Such questions as the following are involved:

1. What constitutes proof for different maturity levels?
    a. Can children be led to discover that when 4 and 3 are added the result is 7 or should they be told this result and be expected to memorize it?
    b. What is the effect of memorization in the early grades on the pupil's ability to think critically and independently at later maturity levels?
    c. How does the concept of proof for a pupil in the seventh grade differ from that for a pupil in the twelfth grade?
    d. What is the degree of complexity of situations involving proof that are best suited to different maturity levels?

These are but segments of the whole problem of proof as it affects the thinking of the young people in our secondary schools.

There have been in the past many efforts to relate mathematics to other areas of learning and to justify the study of mathematics in the senior high school on the ground that the skills thus acquired were helpful in widening the educational horizon of the pupils. While there may be some validity to these claims, it seems to the writer that when the emphasis is on method rather than on skills mathematics can make its greatest contribution to the general education of young people. The ability to express ideas concisely and accurately, the ability to abstract from a situation those qualities which make it different from other situations, the ability to define and the ability to generalize are all recognized as educational values which are common to many areas of learning. This suggests the possibility of the mathematics teacher working in close relation with the language teacher, the social studies teacher and the science teacher, each of whom emphasizes these values from a particular point of view. The problem of using mathematics in the senior high school as illustrative of a powerful method of thought is one which calls for continued and patient research.

The usual tests in mathematics are designed to measure the degree to which the pupil controls the skills which he has been taught. New instruments of evaluation are needed to measure the degree to which the pupil controls and uses the method of thought with which he has become acquainted through the study of proof. Much progress has already been made in this direction through a comprehensive evaluation program which is being directed by Dr. Ralph W. Tyler of Ohio State University. Objective tests dealing with certain aspects of proof have been constructed and are now available. Others are in process of preparation. Through wide use of tests such as these, followed by a careful study of results, worth-while values are likely to receive more emphasis than at present, instruction will become more effective, the tests themselves will be improved and a more comprehensive program of evaluation will be possible.

APPENDIX

PART I

THE following test dealing with the ability of the pupil to analyze non-mathematical material was given to the pupils in classes A, B, C, and D. The results of this test are shown in Table 10, page 103.

1. George came home early from glee club practice at school and picked up the newspaper. In one of the advertisements he saw a picture of Bing Crosby and a package of Old Gold cigarettes. Beneath the picture was this statement,

"My Throat Is My Fortune. . . . That's Why
I Smoke Old Golds," says Bing Crosby.

What facts would have to be proved before this advertisement would influence you to smoke Old Golds? List these facts in the space below.

(Space was left here for this purpose.)

2. Before an election each political party plans and publishes its program. Each program expresses the attitude and plans of that political party if its candidates are elected. These programs help the voters in deciding for whom they will vote at the election. Any party program contains certain key words which should be defined before the program can be clearly understood. Below is a part of one political party's program on the Attitude of Government. Read through this part of the program and select the important words which you think should be clearly defined in order really to understand the program. Write those words in the space below.

"Attitude of Government"

"We propose that the state of Ohio shall be run in the interests of the taxpayers and working people, farmers, and our legitimate business institutions. Political bosses will not be permitted to control the operations of the state government. We are definitely committed to a state program conducted exclusively in the interests of the masses. We pledge ourselves to three general principles:

"First: a prompt, businesslike, economical administration.

"Second: the spirit of genuine service to the public through all the departments of the state government.

"Third: a sympathetic understanding of the problems of the people, and a thoroughly human program to meet these problems insofar as government may be able to do so."

123

On the lines below write the important words or phrases which you think should be clearly defined in order to really understand this political program.

(Space was left for this purpose.)

3. The following quotation was taken from an article published in a magazine. Read it and pick out the main topic that the author has written about and the main ideas which he has stated relative to the main topic.

"The people of Ohio have always regarded public education as a matter of paramount importance. The pioneers who framed Ohio's first Constitution in 1802 incorporated therein a declaration from the Ordinance of 1787: 'Religion, morality, and knowledge being necessary to good government and the happiness of mankind, schools and the means of education shall forever be encouraged.'

"In our present fundamental law, the Constitution adopted in 1851, education is declared in no uncertain terms to be a function of the State government. Section 2 of Article VI reads as follows: 'The General Assembly shall make such provisions, by taxation or otherwise, as will secure a thorough and efficient system of common schools throughout the state.'

"Today Ohio's educational system is a makeshift. School funds in many districts barely suffice for a few months' term at most. Teachers are frequently employed on a three or four-month contract, and their salaries often remain unpaid for many months. The laborer is worthy of his hire, and wages should be paid when wages are due. There should never be an unpaid teacher in Ohio. There should never be a closed school house in Ohio during the regular school term.

"In my opinion, education is a primary function of the state, just as the protection of life, property, and public health are primary functions. Protection must necessarily come first, because without protection of life and property there is no government; but education should come next, because without education popular government cannot long endure. Good roads, for example, are necessary and should be economically built and maintained; but schools come before roads, because education is a primary function of government. Many other objects of expenditure besides roads are often given precedence over educational expenditures. This policy is wrong; government should first discharge its primary functions; no expenditures except those for protection should have precedence over those for education."

What is the main topic that the author has written about?

(Space was left for answer.)

What are the main ideas which he has stated relative to this main topic? Write them here.

(Space was left for this purpose.)

4. Margaret's family have remarked occasionally about how thin her brother Bill is. One day while reading the newspaper Margaret noticed some cartoons showing a thin man. The cartoons also showed that a physician gave the thin man some "Ironized Yeast" to eat regularly. At the end of three months he weighed more and was no longer thin. Margaret showed this to her brother and told him that he ought to eat "Ironized Yeast" so that he would get stouter.

What facts would have to be proved before you would believe that if Bill followed Margaret's advice, he would get stouter? Write them here.

(Space was left for this purpose.)

Bill's family evidently wish him to get stouter. Show how good you think Margaret's advice for making Bill stouter is by rating it, excellent, good, fair, poor, or very poor, whichever word describes it best.

Rating_____

5. While reading a handbill advertisement of a clothing store, Mary noticed this statement: "We sell standard goods for less than our competitors do, because our store is not in the high rent district."

Below is a list of nine statements. In the first column of parentheses, place a plus mark after each statement which you think is taken for granted in the advertisement.

	Col. 1	Col. 2
a. Our competitors charge more than we do for standard goods.	( )	( )
b. It is necessary for a store to charge more for its goods as the rent increases.	( )	( )
c. The only influence which causes the same goods to be sold at different prices is the cost of rent.	( )	( )
d. We charge less for all standard goods.	( )	( )
e. A store which sells for cash can charge less for its goods.	( )	( )
f. All our competitors are in the high rent district.	( )	( )
g. Our volume of business permits us to undersell our competitors.	( )	( )
h. We always sell as low as we can.	( )	( )
i. "Standard goods" give evidence about the quality of the goods.	( )	( )

Read the statements again and in the second column of parentheses, place a plus mark (+) after each statement which is taken for granted in the advertisement and which you believe is probably true.

Place a minus mark (–) in the parentheses after each of the statements which is taken for granted in the advertisement but which you think is probably not true.

The following test in formal geometry was prepared by the teacher of class B and was given to both classes A and B at the end of the first year:

1. Two right triangles are congruent if a side and an acute angle of one triangle are equal respectively to a side and an acute angle of the other.
2. If two angles of a triangle are equal, the sides opposite the angles are equal and the triangle is isosceles.
3. If one pair of opposite sides of a quadrilateral are equal and parallel, the quadrilateral is a parallelogram.
4. If the diagonals of a quadrilateral bisect each other, the figure is a parallelogram.
5. Construct a line making an angle of 60° with a given line.
6. If the base BC of an isosceles triangle ABC is extended so that BD equals CE, then angle ADB equals angle AEC.
7. The lines connecting the mid-points of the sides of a quadrilateral is a parallelogram.
8. In the parallelogram $ABCD$, DC and BA are produced equal lengths to F and E respectively. Prove that EF bisects the diagonal DB.

A copy of the April, 1936, Ohio Every Pupil Test* in plane geometry is shown in the accompanying insert.

PART II

Reference was previously made to papers which the students prepared on "The Evolution of Proof." The mathematics teacher with the assistance of the English teacher selected two of the best, two which were considered average in quality, and two which were poorest in quality. These six papers are presented here, just as they were written by the pupils.

1. THE SEARCH FOR TRUTH
(A Pageant)

(The Stage is dark. From the darkness comes the voice of truth)

Truth—I am truth. I am everywhere, yet you have never found me. I am your greatest potential slave, yet you have never harnessed me. For years you lived and died without realizing my existence or questioning me. It was not until your problems became more complex that you began to search for me. This search, that began in ancient Egypt, has continued up to the present and will not be fulfilled until the thought of man shall become absolutely pure: without prejudice; without emotion.

* * * * * *

*Published by permission of the Ohio Scholarship Tests of the State Department of Education, Columbus, Ohio.

DIRECTIONS	
he Pupil:	
swer the easiest parts first.	
ck and work on the others.	
ll have exactly 40 minutes.	
he Teacher:	
ease return your Form 2 and	
4 report. The results will	
t you and your students.	

EVERY PUPIL TEST, APRIL, 1936

CONDUCTED BY

THE STATE DEPARTMENT OF EDUCATION

COLUMBUS, OHIO

PLANE GEOMETRY

Constructed by

EDITH S. SAUER, Roosevelt High School, Dayton, Ohio

Part I (20)	....
Part II (30)	....
Part III (12)	....
Part IV (18)	....
Score (80)	....

.... Age .... Grade .... Date ....

1 .... Town .... State ....

PART I   SCORE = RIGHTS (20) (........)

Vocabulary

TIONS: Read the following statements and
 on each blank to the right the word which
 added will make the statement true. In
 example, the missing word is "angle",
 "angle" is written on the blank to the

1e: A figure formed
 o straight lines
 from the same vertex
 (an)   ...angle...

o angles whose sum
 ninety degrees are   1.................

straight line touch-
 g the circle in one,
 d only one, point
 a (an)   2.................

closed curve all
 ints of which are
 uidistant from a
 int within, called
 e center, is a (an)   3.................

lygons which are
 tually equiangular
 d whose correspond-
 g sides are propor-
 onal are   4.................

straight line of
 definite length
 ich cuts the circle
 two points is a
 n)   5.................

general geometric
 atement to be proved
 a (an)   6.................

angle whose vertex
 es on a circle and
 ose sides are chords
 the circle is a
 n) ___ angle.   7.................

straight line which
 ins any two points
 a circle and passes
 rough the center is
 (an)   8.................

9. An angle formed by two
 radii at the center of
 the circle is called
 a (an) ___ angle.   9.................

10. An equality between
 two equal ratios is a
 (an)   10.................

11. A polygon of eight
 sides is called a (an)   11.................

12. A parallelogram one of
 whose angles is a
 right angle is a (an)   12.................

13. A line joining two
 non-consecutive
 vertices of a polygon
 is a (an)   13.................

14. An angle whose sides
 extend in opposite
 directions from the
 vertex so as to form
 a straight line is
 called a (an) ___
 angle.   14.................

15. A perpendicular from
 any vertex to the
 opposite side of a
 triangle is a (an)   15.................

16. Three or more lines
 which pass through
 the same point are   16.................

17. A quadrilateral hav-
 ing two, and only two,
 of its sides parallel
 is a (an)   17.................

18. If two lines meet
 forming equal adjacent
 angles, the lines are
 said to be   18.................

19. A rectangle having
 two adjacent sides
 equal is a (an)   19.................

20. A polygon of five
 sides is a (an)   20.................

(Over)

DIRECTIONS: Study the following figures and the given facts and compute the answers as indicated. Answer may be left in radical form or expressed in the nearest tenth. (This necessitates working the problem to two decimal places.) Place the answers on the blanks to the left.

Given: Quad. ABCD inscribed in a circle,
∠ D = 90°, ∠ C = 103°.

.........° 21. ∠ A = ?

.........° 22. ∠ B = ?

Given: △ ABC with DE ∥ AB, CD=4, AD=12, CE=2.

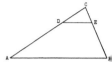

.... 29. EB = ?

Given: Secants AD and AE cutting the circle at B and C respectively, ∠ A=28°, B̂Ĉ=24°.

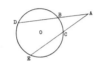

.........° 23. D̂E = ?

Given: △ ABC similar to △ A'B'C',
AB = 6, BC = 4, AC = 8, A'B' = 12.

.... 30. B'C' = ?

Given: Chords DE and EF are equal to the radius of the circle.

.........° 24. ∠ E = ?

.........° 25. ∠ D = ?

Given: △ ABC with ∠ C a right angle,
CD ⊥ AB, AD = 4, AB = 20.

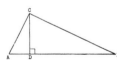

.... 31. CD = ?

.... 32. AC = ?

.... 33. BC = ?

Given: AB is a diameter of circle O. Chords DB and AC are drawn intersecting each other at E. ∠ DEA = 56°.

.........° 26. ∠ COD = ?

Given: Right △ ABC, BC = 7, AC = 24.

.... 34. AB = ?

Given: Regular pentagon ABCDE.

.........° 27. ∠ X = ?

.........° 28. ∠ Y = ?

Given: Isosceles right △ ABC, AB = 12.

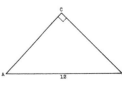

.... 35. AC = ?

Problems on Congruence and Similarity

ECTIONS: In the following problems you are to study the figure, what is given, and what is to be
ved. Then study the solution of each problem. Preceding the problems are given eight reasons that
ly in the proof. On the blank to the right, place the number of the one reason which correctly explains
statement asked for in each problem.

SONS: Two triangles are congruent if:
1. Side, angle, side = side, angle, side.
2. Side, side, side = side, side, side.
3. Angle, side, angle = angle, side, angle.
4. Hypotenuse and acute angle = hypotenuse and acute angle.
5. Hypotenuse and side = hypotenuse and side.

Two triangles are similar if:
6. Two angles of the one are equal respectively to two angles of the other.
7. An angle of one equals an angle of the other, and the including sides are proportional.
8. Three sides of the one are respectively proportional to the three sides of the other.

---

ven: Parallelogram ABCD. K is the midpoint of BC.
AK produced intersects DC produced at E.

prove: △ AKB ≅ △ KCE.

y is the △ AKB ≅ △ KCE?   36...........

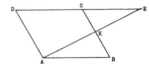

---

ven: △ ABC with AD = DB, ED = DF, DE ⊥ AC, DF ⊥ CB.

prove: △ AED ≅ △ BFD.

y is △ AED ≅ △ BFD?   37...........

---

ven: Isosceles △ ABC, DE = AD.

prove: △ ADE ~ △ ABC.

y is △ ADE ~ △ ABC?   38...........

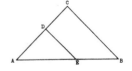

---

ven: AB is a diameter, BC is a tangent to AB at B.

prove: △ ABD ~ △ ABC.

y is △ ABD ~ △ ABC?   39...........

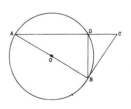

(Over)

CONSTRUCTIONS

DIRECTIONS: You are to make certain formal constructions in the following exercises. Use compasses and straight edge, and leave all construction lines, arcs, etc., in the completed figure.

40. Locate the center of the circle whose arc is AB.

43. Inscribe a circle in the △ ABC.

41. Construct a tangent to circle O from the external point P.

44. Find all points equidistant from two given points, A and B, and also equidistant from two given parallel lines, CD and EF.

P.

42. Divide the line-segment AB into three equal parts.

45. Construct the altitude from C to the side AB in △ ABC.

A ——————————— B

1. THE SEARCH FOR TRUTH (*Continued*)

(The lights come on slowly. Several Egyptian families are walking to the bank of the Nile after it has flooded their land.)

1st Egyptian Man—I will have a good harvest. When the tax-collectors come this year I will have no fear for I will have plenty to give them and yet leave much for myself and my family.

2nd Egyptian Man—You are right neighbor, the Gods have favored us well this year with such rich soil, but the flood was late and we must hurry with the crops if we want them to be harvested when the tax-collectors come.

To start with let us divide our land the way it was before the flood, so that we will each be able to plan our fields.

1st Egyptian Man—That will be easy. I remember well. The dividing line started from the river and went to about where you are standing, then turned and went to where my daughter is standing and went back to the river. I remember the shape and size of my own field.

2nd Egyptian Man—Not well enough if you think it was the size of the one you just cut out. Such a boundary line would give you all of your original land plus most of mine. The line between our fields was over there.

1st Egyptian Man—You forget neighbor that my field always was larger than yours. If anything, the line I laid out would give you some of my land.

2nd Egyptian Man—I see it now, you miserable cheat. You have been planning this trick to cheat me out of my land. You were not satisfied with what you had so you used the flood as a means to take away from me the little land my father gave me. But I will not let you take away my land, you—(he has taken from his clothes a dagger and he stabs the other Egyptian who falls to the ground dead). (His wife and children come and kneel beside him, crying.) (After a minute, one of the sons rises and walks away, looking towards the Nile river.)

The Son—There must be some way to stop this foolish wastefulness of time and life. If only I could find the way to stop it. If only these farmers would agree—Why, that is the answer! Surely, it is possible to make these men agree on a few basic principles and from these it should be simple to make laws of measurement which would decide how men are to divide their land. I must go talk to these farmers and even to Amenenhit. I know these men will realize the importance to their own welfare to agree on these statements. And when I take these statements to Amenenhit, his scholars will be able to find the laws that are implied within them.

BLOCKOUT

Truth—That boy held within his mind one of the first great conceptions of truth. That conception is *agreeing to agree* then producing a set of rules on which all sane men could agree and get the same results at

1. THE SEARCH FOR TRUTH (*Continued*)

all times and in all places. To this day few men have that conception but those who do, think in higher planes than their fellowmen who still use the type of thinking employed by the Egyptian farmers years ago.

That boy took his thinking to Amenenhit and his scholars. But these men did not have the ability to understand fully the great concept that boy presented to them. But Amenenhit did understand enough of the practical implications to have his scholars make certain mathematical laws that he wrote down. Other rulers followed his example and for hundreds of years man accepted the mathematical laws laid down by his rulers as true. What a disheartening road for the Search for Truth to take after such a great start.

*   *   *   *   *   *

But, beginning about 600 B.C. man's thought again rose and reached its first great peak. Up to this time man had not thought to prove his mathematical laws. But Thales started this new concept by proving six very simple and practical theorems that men had been using for years. It was Pythagoras though, who definitely broke away from the practical side of the subject and reached the first great peak in the Searth for Truth.

(The lights slowly come on and Pythagoras is found standing in the center of the stage. Around him stand several men.)

Pythagoras—I demand PROOF!

One of the men—What do you mean proof? Is it not self-evident that these theorems are true?

Pythagoras—What is truth? (No answer.) I can stand here and say that these theorems are false and you can do nothing. You have no weapon to fight a man that has proof. And you can have proof if you will but train your minds in the laws of logic.

Men (Coming up to Pythagoras)—You are right, Pythagoras. Train our minds in the laws of logic. Let us establish a brotherhood. *We shall have proof!* (As they speak the mystic pentagon, the five pointed star, appears in the background.)

Pythagoras—We shall lay down certain postulates which we cannot prove but which we shall all accept. Then a statement shall be said to be proved when, and only when, the statement follows from the postulates by an application of the rules of logic.

BLOCKOUT

Truth—From this beginning Pythagoras and his followers studied the properties of parallel lines, evolved a geometric algebra based on equivalent areas, worked with the five regular solids, and developed a theory of proportion which was discarded with the discovery of incommensurable quantities.

*   *   *   *   *   *

1. THE SEARCH FOR TRUTH (*Continued*)

Truth—Following Pythagoras were two men who helped hold thought in the realm where Pythagoras had put it. Plato inscribed across the entrance to his Academy "Let no one ignorant of geometry enter here." Aristotle made his three laws of logic: A is A; Everything is either A or not A; Nothing is both A and not A. These laws have been accepted as truths for hundreds of years and have only recently been questioned.

*   *   *   *   *   *

Truth—At the close of this period of thought, around 300 B.C. there appeared a man named Euclid who thought he was helping the Search for Truth, but who in reality tied it up so tightly that it stopped and remained motionless for hundreds of years.

(The lights come on showing Euclid seated at a table.)

Euclid—I have much knowledge which will be lost unless I can make a record of it. I will make such a record that will show the findings of other men, that have made possible my work. These shall be my Elements. Thirteen Elements will completely cover all geometric knowledge.

(He begins to write. As he writes the lights dim slowly. Before they go completely out Euclid stops writing.)

Euclid—I have finished. The search is over. There is no geometric knowledge that I have not presented here. For the first time the work of all the great mathematicians has been presented in a logical form without a flaw. THIS IS TRUTH!

(The lights go out.)

(An organ begins to play a slow steady hymn. A monotonous voice chants, "This is true. This is not true. This is true. This is not true, etc." Another one chants, "You must do this. You must not do this. You must do this. You must not do this, etc." Another voice says, "Yours is not to question. Yours is to believe." A voice, very softly at first, begins repeating, "Why? Why? Why? Why? Why? etc." It steadily increases until, with one last shout, it breaks the bonds holding it and the organ and the other voices stop.)

(The lights come on.)

Truth—The bonds are broken: the search goes on! Rene Descartes was one of the first men who began asking why. A reserved, slightly cynical man of the world, he spent his life struggling with many phases of thought. His struggling mind was magnificent and it left its imprint on many fields of thought.

(Rene Descartes is found sitting in his bed.)

Descartes—Why is it not possible to devise a method which would *prove* (or disprove, if false) any known or conjectured theorem in geometry no matter how complicated, by a purely mechanical process?

1. THE SEARCH FOR TRUTH (*Continued*)

I will rob geometry of its frozen repulsiveness and transform it into a living creative science.

I shall replace verbal and logical arguments by mathematical symbols and mathematical operations.

BLOCKOUT

Truth—Men like Descartes broke the bonds and freed men's minds to continue the search. Again thought rose, and reached the second great peak. This peak was reached in 1826: the man responsible for it was Nikolas Ivanovitch Lobatchewsky.

(The lights come on to their full brightness. Lobatchewsky stands on a great pile of chains and ropes, a few of which are tied around his hands.)

Lobatchewsky—I will challenge an axiom of Euclid and nothing will stop me.

Voices from under the chains—The truth of Euclid is eternal. Man has accepted the space of Euclid as the only space. We shall stop you from challenging an axiom of Euclid.

Lobatchewsky—You can not stop me! (A pause) I say there can be more than one straight line drawn through a given point parallel to a given straight line. (Another pause.) You see, you could not stop me. Nothing can stop man's thought. I have made a new space. A space no truer than Euclid's but just as true, just as consistent, and created just as logically. (As Lobatchewsky speaks the chains that held his hands fall off and he stands free, at the top of the pile of chains.)

Truth—(As he speaks more chains fall away and men appear. Men who now stand as Lobatchewsky, not tied by their chains but freed of them.) Lobatchewsky taught men to question. He taught men there was no absolute truth and that any axiom can be challenged. "Truth" was replaced by "consistency" and "human convenience." As man questioned himself and his fellowmen the Search for Truth marched on magnificently.

BLOCKOUT

* * * * * *

Truth—But, another great phase of truth, that of logic, had also lain dormant for years. Man had not thought to question Aristotle's three laws of logic. The first man to question any of these laws was Brouwer. (The lights come on, showing Brouwer.)

Brouwer—I challenge Aristotle's "law" of excluded middle. I do not believe everything is A or not A.

BLOCKOUT

Truth—The second man to challenge these laws was Korzybski. (The lights come on showing Korzybski.)

1. THE SEARCH FOR TRUTH (*Continued*)

Korzybski—I challenge Aristotle's "law of identity." I do not believe that A is always A.

BLOCKOUT

Truth—Aristotle's "law of contradiction" has not been openly questioned as yet. The questioning of the different laws of logic was brought to a peak by Jan Lucasiewicz who with A. Tarski published in 1930 a sufficiently full account of his "many-valued truth-systems."

Now as man goes on to reach greater peaks in his Search for Truth he knows the limitations of his own powers. He knows that he can not find absolute truth. He knows that something is true only as long as it complies and fits into his civilization.

When man progressed from a state of false security and acceptance into a state of question, struggle and change he made a great advance in his Search for Truth; the Search that will continue as long as man has the power to think.

2. EVOLUTION OF PROOF

When one speaks of history or the development of an idea one usually assumes that prior to the first documents of the past that we have there was no civilization as we think of a civilization. This may be true, yet I think it is necessary to realize that there were many centuries during which men lived and thought and it may well be that the ideas we have now concerning proof and its evolution were considered and our conclusions may be merely reiterances of theirs, those ancients whose records were destroyed by wind and time.

In Egypt, for example, we have no knowledge of their earliest civilization. The things we do know concerning them have been gleaned from their papyrus and are very few. One outstanding accomplishment is theirs and it may be inevitable in any human society; that is: common agreement in matters of measurement. In other words it is necessary to set up rules which, when men use them, will lead all men in all places to the same conclusions. Of course, it is impossible for all men in all places to come to the same agreements and conclusions, but it is important that there was an attempt made in Egypt to set up such a set of rules. This assumption dealing with all men agreeing to certain rules is the major assumption back of many of our laws, if not all of them. The Egyptians may not have realized what they were doing. Practical necessity drove them to this perhaps unconsciously.

The Egyptian contribution to the logic of mankind is small in comparison to that of the Greek. The Greeks realized that there was "deductive reasoning" at the back of all common agreements; furthermore, that all this reasoning rests on assumptions, assumptions made by men but believed infallible by the Greeks. Therein lay their biggest fault. They accepted the assumptions they laid down as the only assumptions. They were unable to doubt.

2. EVOLUTION OF PROOF (*Continued*)

The early Greeks had two schools of reasoning; the continuous, or the conception of a universe in a straight line, not broken up into individual parts; discrete, or the belief that the universe was broken up into many definite pieces. These two assumptions have influenced thinking till the present day, e.g. the atomic theory, based on the discrete theory of the universe. These two schools of thought with their respective, conflicting assumptions demonstrate the important influence Greek assumptions have had on our own philosophies. The Greeks believed that it was possible to construct a theory of the universe by deductive reasoning based on a few (*or one*) assumptions. They felt keenly the necessity for truth and they were certain that there was only one truth if it could be found.

The men who left this profound influence with us were many. The first Greek to prove theorems although his object was practical rather than abstract, was Thales who lived from 640 to 546 B.C. He did not rely solely on intuition for coming to conclusions about practical problems.

In or around 569 B.C. a man was born who insisted on proof. He was not as clear on the definition as people came to be later on but he felt it to be dimly this: Certain assumptions, agreed upon, which lead to a conclusion by the applied laws of logic. He felt subconsciously the great need for proof in order to reach common conclusions from the same set of data. Today we study a theorem called by his name, the Pythagorean theorem. But his greatest achievement, assuming that the ultimate of human thinking is the power to understand men's conclusions, was his demand for proof, as he thought of it.

Democritus, who lived about a century after Pythagoras, believed it was futile to seek a proof by finite means. It seemed to him imperative to consider the infinite in reaching a conclusion.

When histories are read and studied, one is certain to come across the names of Aristotle and Euclid. Scientifically and mathematically they are the most important of the Greek philosophers. Aristotle lived before Euclid and he laid down the three laws of thought which were enough to keep people from thinking about proof, logic and truth for 1,000 years. These three laws were, briefly; A is A, everything is either A or not A, nothing is both A and not A. These three assumptions were regarded as laws by the Greeks.

Then in 330 B.C. Euclid was born. He lived fifty-five years and the assumptions he believed in during those fifty-five years, three centuries before the birth of Christ, are the accepted assumptions in most schools and have been ever since he lived. Those that have questioned him have had little effect on the average person's intelligence. The fact that people did finally question him is, however, vastly important. But when Euclid lived the Greeks accepted his assumptions as "self evident" truths and they have been similarly accepted ever since.

"Definitions of Euclid do not always define. Axioms are not always

2. EVOLUTION OF PROOF (*Continued*)

indemonstrable. Demonstrations require many axioms of which he is quite unconscious."[1] Euclid wrote thirteen books and called them the "Elements." They are the organization and summary of the theorems and knowledge of geometry up to that time with a few things, of prime importance, added by Euclid himself.[2] The concepts needed in each book were placed and defined at the beginning of each book. Postulates, or assumptions, were also placed at the beginning of each book. Also, he had placed near the front, "axioms" which were "Self evident assumptions" *and therefore indisputable*, according to Euclid.

Euclid and the Greeks gave us a good many fine things, but they left us with the inability to think in terms of more than one cardinal assumption concerning deductive reasoning.

After Euclid's death in 275 B.C. there is little to be told for several centuries. During the Middle Ages there were three gods worshipped by the people of Western Europe, the Christian God, Aristotle, and Euclid. None of these gods was to be questioned; their words, whether in the Bible or the Elements, were never to be doubted.

However, from the 16th century onward there was a gradual change in all thinking. In the four hundred years since that century there has grown up not only a new conception of proof, but a new conception of science, religion and life. Revolutions really began after the Dark Ages.

Descartes was a Frenchman who lived in the 16th century, the dawn of reasoning. He evolved a method which would enable anyone to prove or disprove any known theorem by a purely mechanical process. He used mathematical symbols and operations instead of what had hitherto been used, i.e. verbal, logical arguments.

It is a little ironical that the first man to show the discrepancies in Euclid's thinking was really attempting to show the infallibility of the assumptions and proved conclusions of Euclid's. Saccheri was a Jesuit priest, who lived from 1667–1733. He had been a careful student of Euclid and he felt himself capable to clear up some of Euclid's work and demonstrate the truth of it. He assumed one of the postulates false and then proceeded to show that the conclusion became an absurdity. His work now shows that he pointed out unconsciously the weaknesses of Euclid.

But it was not until the 19th century that simultaneously two men not only challenged Euclid, but established doubt. Bolyai, in 1823, announced to some friends that he had constructed a new geometry, with different assumptions and conclusions, which proved to be as logical as Euclid's. He changed one major assumption, that one which says one and only one line can be drawn through a point parallel to a given line, and a new geometry was born.

[1] Eric T. Bell, *The Search for Truth*, p. 126. Bertrand Russell quoted. Williams and Wilkins Co., Baltimore.

[2] Vera Sanford, *Short History of Mathematics*, p. 269. Houghton Mifflin Co., Boston, 1926.

2. EVOLUTION OF PROOF (*Continued*)

Almost at the same time, in Russia, Lobachevsky challenged the assumption that one and only one line can be drawn through a given point parallel to a given line. He changed the dogmatic assertions of truth, hitherto expressed, to words like "consistency" and "human convenience" when speaking of logic and truth. Man no longer sought the truth of the gods, he merely sought consistency in terms of human assumptions. Truth became what we make it, subject to change of any kind. Anyone can manufacture any geometry for any purpose by laying down any assumptions or changing any assumptions already made.

During the course of the 19th and 20th centuries several men considered Aristotle's laws inconsistent and showed their weaknesses. The complete overthrow of the gods was almost complete.

Two of Aristotle's laws had been challenged, those first two: A is A and everything is either A or not A. There remained only one pillar, the foundations of which were so firm in the Dark Ages, but which shook and fell when two Polish gentlemen by the names of Lucasiewicz and Tarski in 1930 showed that the old law of every proposition being either true or not true was not complete. They showed that good *workable* deductive systems can be created in which propositions can be true or not true, or any other number of values different from these.

This brings the evolution of proof down to the present day and the modern concept. In stating a proposition today we take into account the fact that some material is given us. If such and such is true, then the proposition follows by inference. All proof rests on certain undefined terms. As few as possible terms must be defined because out of these few workable "undefinables" come the defined terms, the assumptions and finally the conclusion. The defined terms and the assumptions must, for clarity, follow from the undefined terms first stated and must bear directly on the proposition to be proved. Thus, if certain things be, then a conclusion follows. The "if" part of the statement and the conclusion may both be false to some ways of thinking but the assertion in that form would be true.

This, I believe, is the crux of this search. Man is limited by his own senses. His own assumptions concerning the world about him are all he has. Therefore the conclusions he comes to from those assumptions may be *any* conclusions because each individual makes his own particular assumptions. Truth may be found by every man because in every man's mind lies the truth.

BIBLIOGRAPHY

Bell, Eric T. *The Search for Truth.* Williams and Wilkins Co., New York, 1926.
Keyser, C. J. *Thinking about Thinking.* Dutton and Co., New York, 1926.
Sanford, Vera. *Short History of Mathematics.* Houghton Mifflin Co., Boston, 1926.

3. CONCEPT OF PROOF TODAY

It appears to me at the present time that there is no logical reason that I should attempt to do what I imagine most of the students are doing, for their final paper of this year. They believe they are concluding their course in Geometry and the Nature of Proof, and that, in my estimation, is exactly what they are doing, nothing more or less. The present conception of a high school course demands that there be a conclusion and also a definite date for such a conclusion. I like to believe that I am writing another chapter in view of a closer understanding of the Nature of Proof. There is no reason why the average student should write a paper as a conclusion to a subject. Instead each successive writing should open the gates of that subject a little wider to him and permit him to enter without as much difficulty as before.

I.

The history of geometry has been traced back to originating with the Egyptians. The Egyptians had, for the most part, only applied geometry, that is geometry that seemed to solve their practical problems at hand. They accepted these solutions, evidently without much question, and made little attempt to prove them.

Thales, a Greek (640–546 B.C.) studied the improved geometry of the Egyptians and attempted to prove some of the theorems instead of merely accepting them. Thales work contributed materially to Euclid's Elements, about 300 years later.

Pythagoras (572–501 B.C.) was a philosopher who worked towards the theory of geometry instead of the practical side. Pythagoras is usually credited with the discovery of the theorems concerning the sum of the angles of a triangle and of polygons. There is a doubt, however, in the minds of many mathematicians as to whether Pythagoras was the discoverer of the theorem of the 3–4–5 right triangle, or not. David Eugene Smith says that the relation of the sides of a triangle was well known long before the time of Pythagoras. Documental evidence was found that led to the belief that the Chinese had stated the theorem. The Egyptians knew a similar relation and "Pythagorean" numbers were used in India. The belief that Pythagoras proved this theorem rests solely on tradition and there exists no record of how he proved it.

Euclid's Elements are a summarization of the mathematical knowledge of his time. All geometrical proofs are given in formal form and are often followed by a statement of conditions under which the problem is impossible to prove.

The invention of the printing press in Europe about 1480 was the factor which first made the works of Euclid widely known. For a time in the 17th century analytic geometry took much of the interest from the older geometry until later times.

Many writers have attacked the 4th and 5th postulates of Euclid and

3. CONCEPT OF PROOF TODAY (*Continued*)

have attempted to demonstrate proofs for these postulates. Many of these demonstrated proofs were found to be fallacious. Proclus offered an alternate to postulate 5, i.e., through a given point only one parallel can be drawn to a given straight line.

Euclid's *Elements* contain most of the basic theorems in elementary plane geometry. Most of the material in the *Elements* is the work of men other than Eulcid; in fact, Euclid contributed very little original work to the mathematical world.

Before Euclid the work with parallel lines contained many contradictions. Euclid removed these contradictions by stating his famous fifth postulate, i.e., straight lines, which, being in the same plane and being produced indefinitely in both directions do not meet one another in either direction. Mathematicians did not desire to accept this as a postulate but no one has been able to prove it as a proposition. About 2000 years passed before men realized that this postulate was independent of Euclid's other definitions and assumptions.

Non-Euclidean geometry is any system of geometry whose postulates contradict those of Euclid, especially postulate number 5.

Saccheri (1667–1733) was a Jesuit priest and the first to write of non-Euclidean geometries. It is interesting to note that he did not realize that he was writing on this subject. He wrote a paper which was an attempt to clear Euclid of the criticisms of the parallel line postulate and treatment of proportions. Saccheri assumed postulate 5 false and then showed that such an assumption was absurd. Even though some of Saccheri's work was inconsistent this was not discovered for over a hundred years.

Bolyai (1775–1856) was a friend of Gauss who was making a study of the acute angle hypothesis.[3] In 1823 Janos Bolyai (1802–1860) developed a system of geometry with such conclusions as: in a plane two lines could be drawn through a point parallel to a given line; and that through this point an infinite number of lines might be drawn lying in the angle between the first two and having the property that they would not intersect the given line. Obviously this theorem was in contrast with Euclid but it was considered equally logical.

Nicolai Ivanovitch Lobachevsky (1793–1856) was an obscure Russian who was working on acute angle geometry.[3] His work was not translated until 1840. Gauss was so interested in his work that he thought of studying Russian in order to read the other works of Lobachevsky.

Riemann (1826–1866) developed a geometry in which all lines were of finite length. Any pair of lines intersected if they lay in the same plane, and the sum of the angles of a triangle was greater than two right angles. As Bell states for over 2000 years Euclid had geometry hog-tied so that no one thought of any other system. We must realize

[3] Vera Sanford, *A Short History of Mathematics.* "Acute Angle Hypothesis." Bolyai, p. 279, Lobachevsky, p. 280, Saccheri, pp. 276–277.

3. CONCEPT OF PROOF TODAY (*Continued*)

that Euclidean and non-Euclidean geometries are equally logical and both give results much more accurate than the accuracy of our measurements, if such a procedure could be possible.

II

It seems to me that generally there is no concept of proof today among most of our population; by that I mean there is a concept of proof but most people don't know it. This can be readily illustrated if you ask the average person, for instance, why a certain statement is true. That person will say it is true because it is. He doesn't know why it is true and there is little hope for him to develop a logical proof to show that it is true. Many persons can give what they call a proof but the laymen can usually punch holes in each other's proof. Consequently this would make it simple for a logician to tear such an illogical proof to bits.

While in Paris, I told a French Ford dealer that we owned an American Ford. He looked at me strangely as if I had just emerged from an institution and told me that all Fords were English and made in England. What was I to say? All the arguing that I could undertake in French would not persuade him to my belief. My proof was lacking, no logical argument could help. My only possible proof would be his education. I dropped the subject and by so doing I assumed that sometime he would be educated of that fact. I suggest this procedure as a means of evading proof in cases where it is not needed at the moment. One can either trust to luck that the person will become educated to certain facts or one can bring about such education by indirect methods. Besides using indirect education as a way of proving facts, it can also be well used to prove or at least show the existence of some assumptions. While a person is in an argument he will rarely be satisfied to drop the subject and hope the other person or persons will find out later that he was right. It is human nature to turn an argument into a quibble, and then into warfare. We must not lose control of ourselves but must be satisfied to stop some arguments without having reached any conclusion. It starts with people in the home getting into a hot argument and ends up with nations losing their tempers and fighting. The worst of it is that after the fight is all over no conclusions are reached. Usually you are right back where you started from and eagerly waiting to start all over again. Nothing is settled and nothing is proved. There is where education comes in. If people were logically educated, that is progressively educated, they could handle a logical argument and know when to present one, also know when not to bother with presenting one.

I sincerely believe that schools such as ours are on the right track towards a logical education. We are by no means perfect yet, if ever, but we are progressing!

3. CONCEPT OF PROOF TODAY (*Continued*)

BIBLIOGRAPHY

Bell, Eric T. *The Search for Truth.* Williams and Wilkins, Baltimore, 1934.
Keyser, C. J. *Thinking about Thinking.* E. P. Dutton and Co., New York, 1926.
Sanford, Vera. *A Short History of Mathematics.* Houghton Mifflin Co., Boston, 1930.
Smith, David Eugene. *The History of Mathematics.* Vol. 2. Ginn and Co., Boston, 1932.

4. THE EVOLUTION OF PROOF

Proof, as it is known today, has come through many centuries of evolutionary thought and experiment done by men in many places on this world.

The Egyptians, some four or five thousand years ago, were probably the first people to use geometry as a method of solving practical construction problems. In doing this, they laid the foundation for the great structure of abstract proof, started principally by the Greeks.

Thales, between 640 and 546 B.C., studied the applied geometry of the Egyptians, and proved, by abstract and logical thought, many of the geometric theorems which the people of Egypt had used for practical purposes. His lack of contentment to accept these theorems on the basis of intuition or experiment was what started the "ball of proof" rolling.

Thales was more concerned with geometry of lines than with that of areas, the latter being used, as formulas, by the Egyptians. He founded the geometry of lines, and although he used abstract thinking to prove his theorems, he had many practical ends in view.

The first philosopher to make the study of geometry a part of a liberal education was Pythagoras, 572–501 B.C. He definitely broke away from the practical side of the subject. Pythagoras and his followers, who called themselves the Pythagoreans, discovered and proved many valuable theorems. Among them were those relating to the sum of the angles in a triangle, and also the famous Pythagorean Theorem. However, there is some doubt as to whether the Pythagoreans were the first to discover this hypothesis or not, but the credit for the general theorem rightly belongs to them. They were the first to use geometry to express relationships between quantities, and Pythagoras had established proportions, but these, it was discovered, were only valid in the cases of commensurable magnitudes.

The period between Pythagoras and Plato was a very active one along mathematical lines, much thought and experiment being brought about by the innumerable attempts to solve the three famous problems, the trisection of an angle, the duplication of the cube, and the quadrature of the circle.

Although Plato, 429–347 B.C., is better remembered for other phases of his philosophies, he played an important part in the development of

4. THE EVOLUTION OF PROOF (*Continued*)

the geometric proof of his time. Plato wrote over the entrance to his school, "Let no one who is unacquainted with geometry enter here."

Euclid, whose name is most immediately connected with geometry, even today, was born about 365 B.C. He wrote his *Elements* during the period from 330 to 320 B.C. He was extraordinarily skillful in arranging in an orderly and logical manner the mathematics of his day, clearly stating his definitions, assumptions-postulates, etc. Very few of the separate proofs were his own, but his power to organize and systematize all the available knowledge of mathematics, not only geometry, entitles him to the high place which he holds, even today. In spite of this, it seems somewhat evident today that Euclid considered his assumptions the only logical ones, and his resultant conclusions as equally singular and logical. When one realizes that Euclid did not consider other assumptions than those which seemed to be borne out by "apparency," it is obvious that there is some room for doubt as to the "absolute truth" of his conclusions.

Although the Greeks did not consider the many phases and concepts of a proof that we now do, they nevertheless had, by the time of Euclid, established the importance of abstract thinking and proving in the intellectual life of man.

The Romans seemed somewhat content to leave the so-called "abstract philosophies" to the Greeks and a few scholars, and generally use the more practical aspects of geometry in their construction (and destruction) work, much as did the Egyptians.

In Europe, throughout the Middle Ages very little was known of Euclid outside of a few scattered monasteries, universities, and other places of knowledge and learning. Probably more was known at that time about the field of demonstrative geometry by the Arabs than by the Europeans, as they had been among the first to have the *Elements* translated into their language.

Until the early part of the seventeenth century, almost all of the people who knew anything about abstract proof were content to accept the Euclidean geometry, not contesting its "complete and absolute validity."

Saccheri, 1667–1733, a Jesuit priest, in attempting to forever end the very few but irritating criticisms of Euclid's fifth postulate (through a given point, one and only one straight line may be drawn parallel to a given line) unwittingly made known the possibility of forms of geometry other than Euclidean.

In the latter part of the eighteenth century, a Hungarian, Bolyai, and his son, Janos, by questioning the eternal validity of this fifth Euclidean postulate, established an entirely new "world" of geometry. At the same time in Russia, a man called Lobachevsky practically duplicated the reasoning of the Bolyais. One of the "amazing" conclusions reached by these men with their new basis for logical thought, was that the sum of the angles of a triangle is *less* than 180 degrees, not

4. THE EVOLUTION OF PROOF (*Continued*)

the sum of two right angles or 180°, as the Euclidean geometry had concluded.

Another new "world" of geometry, not considered by either the Bolyais or Lobachevsky, was discovered by a German, Riemann. It grows out of the same questionable Euclidean postulate as did the other, but in the case of the sum of the angles of a triangle, the conclusions of Riemann were exactly the opposite of those of the other men! Riemann, through his process of reasoning, found the sum of the angles of a triangle to be *more* than 180 degrees. The discovery of this geometry was undoubtedly delayed by the retention of the Euclidean postulate concerning the length of straight lines.

It must be pointed out that these three geometries have been found to be equally logical in their abstract thought. The main reason for the Euclidean geometry's being so much more widely taught and used is that Euclid's assumptions, *for the most part*, are more readily borne out by practical experience. But in the light of pure abstract and logical proof, where the senses and environments are discounted, the assumptions of all three geometries are valid. Only in their assumptions and definitions do these geometries differ and the logical process of thought is present in all three.

Truly, the chief contribution of men such as Bolyai, Riemann and Lobachevsky has been to show that a conclusion, or a whole system of logic for that matter, is only true to the extent to which one accepts its basic assumptions and definitions as valid. There certainly can be no *absolute truth* when the truth of a truth itself hinges upon so many variable factors.

To the writer, proof today is not conceived of as being limited solely to the area of geometry, but is a process of logical argument, which is carried on with the basic aid of certain assumptions and definitions, and may have as its subject any, or almost any phase of human thought. It is extremely important, however, to point out again that this proof, irregardless of the subject, is directly dependent upon its primary assumptions and definitions for its conclusions or point of view, and it will be accepted only when the thinking person who accepts it agrees with its assumptions and definitions.

BIBLIOGRAPHY

Bell, Eric T. *The Search for Truth*. Williams and Wilkins Co., Baltimore, 1934.
Sanford, Vera. *A Short History of Mathematics*. Houghton, Mifflin Co., Boston, 1930.

5. EVOLUTION OF PROOF

Before the time of 600 B.C. there was no proof what-so-ever. Mathematics was used constantly by the Egyptians when building their pyramids, but they did not attempt to prove their conclusions.

5. EVOLUTION OF PROOF (Continued)

Thales, a Greek philosopher who lived from 640–546 B.C. was the first to use demonstrative geometry. He studied the applied geometry of the Egyptians and started to prove the propositions instead of accepting them on the basis of intuition or experiment. He founded the geometry of lines and laid the foundation of algebra for he established an equation in the true sense of the word. He also laid the foundation of the methods of measurement of heights and distances. He accomplished a great deal in the field of astronomy.

Pythagoras (572–501 B.C.) also a Greek philosopher was the first man to make the study of geometry a part of liberal education. He had a great many followers which united to form the Pythagoreans which were the first to use geometry to express the relationship between quantities. Their definition of proportion applied only to commensurable lines. Their entire concept was discarded when incommensurable lines were discovered to exist, only to be revived when Eudoxus formulated a definition applicable to all cases.

There was great activity in the field of geometry from the time of Pythagoras to Plato. Important mathematicians around that time (500–400 B.C.) were:

Hippocrates who tried to square the circle and was the first to write a systematic treatment of geometry.

Anaxagoras who also worked with squaring the circle.

Hippias who worked with the trisection of an angle.

Theodorous who showed that the square roots of 3, 5, 7 . . . 17 were irrational.

Democritus worked with propositions regarding the volume of cones and pyramids.

Archytas classified the four mathematical sciences, geometry, arithmetic, astronomy and music. He also worked with duplication the cube.

Around this time many men were concerned with the three great problems of geometry which have never been solved by geometry. These problems are: the trisection of an angle, the duplication of a cube, and squaring a circle.

Euclid who lived around 300 B.C. is one of the most important men in geometry. He taught at Alexandria and there wrote his famous books the "Elements." His concepts are defined at the beginning of each of his thirteen books, his postulates and "axioms" are stated. Each proof is given in standardized form. He contributed little in the way of subject matter although that was of prime importance. His work became widely known after the invention of printing.

Non-Euclidean Geometry

Non-Euclidean geometry is any system of geometry whose postulates contradict those of Euclid, although it is usually thought of as disagreeing with Euclid's fifth postulate, that of "one and only one line can be drawn parallel to a given line through a given point."

5. EVOLUTION OF PROOF (Continued)

Saccheri, a Jesuit priest was the first to deal with non-Euclidean geometrics. He was a brilliant Italian teacher with a remarkable memory. He failed to be the founder of non-Euclidean geometry because he did not perceive the possible truth of his non-Euclidean hypotheses. Saccheri took Euclid's famous postulate 5 and assumed it to be false. From this he developed the acute angle and obtuse angle hypotheses.

Bolyai (1775–1856) a Hungarian and his son Janos (1802–1860) developed a new system of geometry on acute angle hypothesis and they made such conclusions as: in a plane, instead of one line, two lines could be drawn through a point parallel to a given line and through this point an infinite number of lines might be drawn lying in the angle between the first two and having the property that they would not intersect the given line.

Lobachewsky (1793–1856) a Russian, lectured on the acute angle geometry at the University of Kazan. He was one of the first thinkers to apply a critical treatment to the fundamental axioms of geometry.

Riemann, a German (1826–1866) also worked on the obtuse angle hypothesis. He developed a geometry in which all lines were of finite length and any pair of lines intersected if they lay in the same plane, and the sum of the angles of a triangle is greater than 180°.

Analytic geometry was created by Rene Descartes and Pierre de Fermat, two Frenchmen. The two main ideas involved are the location of points in a figure by the use of co-ordinates and the algebraic representation of a curve or surface by an equation involving two or three variables.

The concept of proof today is that all of our doctrines are built up on assumptions, definitions and undefined terms and because people's assumptions and definitions differ they disagree in their beliefs. In our concept there is no absolute truth but a doctrine is true within the limits of its assumptions.

In our study of the nature of proof we have tried to discover the underlying assumptions and words that need to be defined before an understanding can be reached in our propositions and those of others.

6. EVOLUTION OF PROOF

Demonstration geometry started with Thales, an ancient Greek of about 600 B.C. Before Thales the geometry of the Greeks was merely intuition. He discovered six theorems and their proofs. He was famous for finding the height of a pyramid from its shadow and a ship's distance from shore. He also made the calculation for the length of a year. None of Thales' theorems were ever written by him. All of his proofs were varied in their subject matter.

Around 572 B.C. Pythagoras started the study of geometry in liberal education. He restrained his study to triangles and polygons. He is famous for the theorem that the square of the hypotenuse of a right triangle equals the sum of the squares of the other two sides.

6. EVOLUTION OF PROOF (*Continued*)

Euclid a Greek of about 300 B.C. wrote his "Elements." He taught at Alexandria. His "Elements" were supposed to be purely geometry, but they also contain algebra. Euclid wrote his "Elements" in very formal style for the highly educated of those days. Euclid had thirteen books in his "Elements." His book is known as the oldest textbook still in use today. Euclid also wrote around twenty-five other geometric propositions on the celestial sphere. As I have mentioned the early geometry was merely symmetric figures in a mat, and not until Thales did proof by deductive reasoning exist

In 1500 B.C. geometry was first written down. In China writings were found showing they knew the relationship of certain right angle triangles. But no proofs were found for these. China however never contributed to the world in the way of geometry.

In India were found many formulated rules, but the thinking was all empirical. The Romans wanted geometry only for the use of laying out cities and engineering projects.

The Greeks were the originators of geometry and they were the people to encourage and build it up. Through Thales' clear demonstrations that he gave for lack of his theorems is laid the blame of so many becoming interested in geometry. Geometry was the Greek's main mathematics.

The Arabs read and translated the Greek geometry, but made no contributions. Geometry came into study by degrees, in 510 Boethius, in 1000 Gerbert, and in 1220 Fibonacci brought geometry back into the rage during each of their lives.

After printing was invented Euclid's book was widely put into use.

Euclid's assumption on parallel lines was disagreed with by many interested mathematicians and Saccheri investigated this, his work aided Lobachevsky. Lobachevsky believed that through a given point more than one parallel line may be drawn to a given line. Bolyai and Lobachevsky were working the same time on this theorem. Riemann was the next outstanding contributor. He favored analytic geometry, suggesting a negative curvature. This differed from Euclid and Bolyai.

In 18th Century

In Germany men such as Heilbronner gave great attention to the science of mathematics.

In France was Jean Etienne Montucla who wrote on the history of mathematics.

In 19th Century

An Italian named Franchini who was a famous teacher and who wrote a little on the history of mathematics.

Arneth a German was a teacher and historian. Hermann Haukel was classed as great and would have done a valuable piece of work had he lived long enough to complete the work he started on the history of all mathematics. He was also a great translator.

6. EVOLUTION OF PROOF (*Continued*)

In this century Denmark possessed a prominent historian by the name of Teuthen. He wrote on Greek mathematics.

Britain also produced a writer Allinan, he wrote the Greek history of Thales. His work was unsurpassed until 1924 by Sir Thomas Heath. The modern concept of proof is based on undefined terms and assumptions, and any assumptions may be made.

BIBLIOGRAPHY

Sanford, Vera. *A Short History of Mathematics*. Houghton Mifflin Co., Boston, 1930.

Smith, David Eugene. *The History of Mathematics*. Vol. 1 and 2, Ginn and Co., Boston, 1925.

BIBLIOGRAPHY

BEATLEY, RALPH. "The Second Report of the Committee on Geometry."
The Mathematics Teacher, Vol. xxvi, No. 6, 1933, pp. 366–371.
BEATLEY, RALPH. "The Third Report of the Committee on Geometry."
The Mathematics Teacher, Vol. xxviii, Nos. 6–7, 1935, pp. 329–450.
BELL, ERIC T. *Men of Mathematics*. Simon and Schuster, New York, 1937.
BELL, ERIC T. *The Queen of the Sciences*. Williams and Wilkins Co.,
Baltimore, 1931.
BELL, ERIC T. *The Search for Truth*. Williams and Wilkins Co., Balti-
more, 1934.
CHRISTOFFERSON, H. C. *A State Wide Survey of the Learning and Teaching
of Geometry*. Ohio State Department of Education, Columbus, 1931.
CHRISTOFFERSON, H. C. *Geometry Professionalized for Teachers*. George
Banta Publishing Co., Menasha, Wis., 1933.
COLUMBIA ASSOCIATES IN PHILOSOPHY. *An Introduction to Reflective
Thinking*. Houghton Mifflin Co., Boston, 1923.
DEWEY, JOHN. *How We Think*. D. C. Heath and Co., Boston, 1910.
HOTELLING, HAROLD. "Some Little Known Applications of Mathematics."
The Mathematics Teacher, Vol. xxix, No. 4, 1936, pp. 157–169.
KEYSER, C. J. "The Human Worth of Rigorous Thinking." *The Mathe-
matics Teacher*, Vol. xv, No. 1, 1922, pp. 1–5.
KEYSER, C. J. *Thinking about Thinking*. E. P. Dutton & Co., New York,
1926.
KILPATRICK, W. H. "The Next Step in Method." *The Mathematics
Teacher*, Vol. xv, No. 1, 1922, pp. 16–25.
LIEBER, LILLIAN. *Three Moons in Mathesis*. Lillian Lieber, 258 Clinton
Ave., Brooklyn, N. Y.
MATHEMATICAL ASSOCIATION. *Report: The Teaching of Geometry in Schools*.
G. Bell & Sons, Ltd., London, 1929.
NATIONAL COMMITTEE ON MATHEMATICAL REQUIREMENTS. *The Re-
organization of Mathematics in Secondary Education*. (Part 1.) Hough-
ton Mifflin Co., Boston, 1923.
NATIONAL COUNCIL OF TEACHERS OF MATHEMATICS. *The Eleventh Year-
book*. Bureau of Publications, Teachers College, Columbia University,
New York, 1936.
NATIONAL COUNCIL OF TEACHERS OF MATHEMATICS. *The Fifth Yearbook*.
Bureau of Publications, Teachers College, Columbia University,
New York, 1930.
NATIONAL COUNCIL OF TEACHERS OF MATHEMATICS. *The Tenth Yearbook*.
Bureau of Publications, Teachers College, Columbia University, New
York, 1935.
PARKER, ELSIE. "Teaching Pupils the Conscious Use of a Technique of

Thinking." *The Mathematics Teacher*, Vol. xvii, No. 4, 1924, pp. 191–201.

PERRY, WINONA. *A Study in the Psychology of Learning in Geometry.* Bureau of Publications, Teachers College, Columbia University, New York, 1925.

REEVE, WILLIAM D. "Research in Mathematics Education." *The Mathematics Teacher*, Vol. xxix, No. 1, 1936, pp. 6–9.

SANFORD, VERA. *A Short History of Mathematics.* Houghton Mifflin Co., Boston, 1930.

SHANHOLT, HENRY H. "A New Deal in Geometry." *The Mathematics Teacher*, Vol. xxix, No. 2, 1936, pp. 67–74.

SHIBLI, J. *Recent Developments in the Teaching of Geometry.* Pennsylvania State College, State College, Pa., 1932.

SLOSSON, EDWIN E. *Easy Lessons in Einstein.* Harcourt, Brace and Co., New York, 1920.

SMITH, DAVID EUGENE. *History of Mathematics.* Vol. 2. Ginn and Co., Boston, 1925.

STABLER, E. RUSSELL. "Teaching an Appreciation of Mathematics: The Need of Reorganization in Geometry." *The Mathematics Teacher*, Vol. xxvii, No. 1, 1934, pp. 30–40.

STAMPER, ALVIN W. *The History of the Teaching of Elementary Geometry.* Bureau of Publications, Teachers College, Columbia University, New York, 1909.

WITTY, PAUL A. "Intelligence: Its Nature, Development and Measurement." Chap. xvi in *Educational Psychology*, edited by Skinner, Charles E. Prentice-Hall, 1936.

YOUNG, J. W. A. *The Teaching of Mathematics in the Elementary and Secondary Schools.* Longmans, Green and Co., New York, 1924. (Revised)